Maria Marcia Fanny Wilson

Devotions before and after Holy Communion

Maria Marcia Fanny Wilson

Devotions before and after Holy Communion

ISBN/EAN: 9783741165061

Manufactured in Europe, USA, Canada, Australia, Japa

Cover: Foto ©Lupo / pixelio.de

Manufactured and distributed by brebook publishing software (www.brebook.com)

Maria Marcia Fanny Wilson

Devotions before and after Holy Communion

DEVOTIONS

BEFORE AND AFTER

HOLY COMMUNION.

Oxford and London:
HENRY AND JAMES PARKER.
1865.

By Miss French.

THIS little Manual, drawn up, it is hoped, in the true spirit of the ancient Liturgies and of our own, is heartily commended to those, who desire and pray to be taught by the Church how best to approach our Lord.

J. K.

Feb. 14, 1865.

BEFORE HOLY COMMUNION.

Before Holy Communion.

MONDAY.

PRAYER FOR HELP DURING PREPARATION.

My duty is to exhort you in the mean season to consider the dignity of that holy mystery, and the great peril of the unworthy receiving thereof; and so to search and examine your own consciences (and that not lightly, and after the manner of dissemblers with God; but so), that ye may come holy and clean to such a heavenly feast, in the marriage-garment required by God in Holy Scripture, and be received as worthy partakers of that holy table.

At Morning Prayer.

In the Name of the Father, and of the Son, and of the Holy Ghost. Amen.

℣. O Lord, open Thou my lips;

℟. And my mouth shall shew forth Thy praise.

℣. O God, make speed to save me;

℟. O Lord, make haste to help me.

BEFORE HOLY COMMUNION.

HYMN.

Bread of the world, in mercy broken,
Wine of the soul, in mercy shed,
By Whom the words of life were spoken,
And in Whose death our sins are dead.

Look on the heart by sorrow broken,
Look on the tears by sinners shed;
And be Thy Feast to us the token
That by Thy grace our souls are fed.

To God the Father adoration,
The Son and Holy Ghost our guide,
As was of old before creation,
Is now, and ever shall abide.   Amen.

Antiphon. Examine me, O Lord, and prove me: try out my reins and my heart.

PSALM 26.   *Judica me, Domine.*

Be thou my judge, O Lord, for I have walked innocently: my trust hath been also in the Lord, therefore shall I not fall.

Examine me, O Lord, and prove me: try out my reins and my heart.

For thy loving-kindness is ever before mine eyes: and I will walk in thy truth.

I have not dwelt with vain persons: neither will I have fellowship with the deceitful.

I have hated the congregation of the wicked: and will not sit among the ungodly.

I will wash my hands in innocency, O Lord: and so will I go to thine altar.

That I may shew the voice of thanksgiving: and tell of all thy wondrous works.

Lord, I have loved the

MONDAY.

habitation of thy house: and the place where thine honour dwelleth.

O shut not up my soul with the sinners: nor my life with the bloodthirsty;

In whose hands is wickedness: and their right hand is full of gifts.

But as for me, I will walk innocently: O deliver me, and be merciful unto me.

My foot standeth right: I will praise the Lord in the congregations.

Glory be, &c.

Ant. Examine me, O Lord.

Chapter. Let your loins be girded about and your lights burning; and ye yourselves like unto men that wait for their lord.— *S. Luke* xii. 35, 36.

Lord, have mercy upon us.
Christ, have mercy upon us.
Lord, have mercy upon us.

Our Father.

Prevent us, O Lord, in all our doings with Thy most gracious favour, and further us with Thy continual help: that in all our works, begun, continued, and ended in Thee, we may glorify Thy holy name, and finally by Thy mercy obtain everlasting life; through Jesus Christ our Lord. Amen.

O Lord my God, I have sinned against Heaven and before Thee, and I am not worthy to be made partaker of Thy immaculate Mysteries; but as a merciful God make me worthy of Thy grace, that without condemnation I may be partaker of Thy holy Body and precious Blood, to forgiveness of sins and life everlasting. Amen.

O Great High Priest, the true Priest, Jesu Christ, Who didst offer Thyself to God the Father a pure and spotless Victim upon the Altar of the Cross for us miserable sinners, and didst give us Thy Flesh to eat and Thy Blood to drink, and didst ordain that Mystery in the Power of Thy Holy Spirit, saying, 'This do in remembrance of Me;' I pray Thee, by that wonderful and unspeakable Love wherewith Thou deignedst so to love us miserable and unworthy, as to wash us from our sins in Thy Blood: teach me, Thine unworthy servant, by Thy Holy Spirit, to approach so great a Mystery with such reverence and honour, devotion and fear, as I ought, and as is fitting. Make me, through Thy grace, always so to believe and understand, to conceive and firmly to hold, to think and to speak, of that exceeding Mystery, as shall please Thee and be good for my soul.

Let Thy good Spirit enter my heart, and there be heard without utterance, and without the sound of words speak all truth. For Thy

Mysteries are exceeding deep, and covered with a sacred veil. For Thy great mercy's sake, grant me to approach Thy holy Mysteries with a clean heart and a pure mind. Free my heart from all defiling and unholy, from all vain and hurtful thoughts. Fence me with the holy and faithful guard and mighty protection of Thy blessed Angels, that the enemies of all good may go away ashamed. By the virtue of this mighty Mystery, and by the hand of Thy holy Angel, drive away from me and from all Thy servants the hard spirit of pride and vainglory, envy and blasphemy, impurity and uncleanness, doubting and mistrust. Let them be confounded that seek after my soul to destroy it; let them perish that seek my hurt.

God the Father, God the Son, God the Holy Ghost, be with me and with mine, now and at the hour of death. Amen.

At Evening Prayer.

In the Name of the Father, and of the Son, and of the Holy Ghost. Amen.

℣. O Lord, open Thou my lips;

℟. And my mouth shall shew forth Thy praise.

BEFORE HOLY COMMUNION.

℣. O God, make speed to save me;
℟. O Lord, make haste to help me.

Antiphon. My soul thirsteth for Thee, my flesh also longeth after Thee.

PSALM 63. *Deus, Deus meus.*

O God, thou art my God: early will I seek thee.

My soul thirsteth for thee, my flesh also longeth after thee: in a barren and dry land where no water is.

Thus have I looked for thee in holiness: that I might behold thy power and glory.

For thy loving-kindness is better than the life itself; my lips shall praise thee.

As long as I live will I magnify thee on this manner: and lift up my hands in thy Name.

My soul shall be satisfied, even as it were with marrow and fatness: when my mouth praiseth thee with joyful lips.

Have I not remembered thee in my bed: and thought upon thee when I was waking?

Because thou hast been my helper: therefore under the shadow of thy wings will I rejoice.

My soul hangeth upon thee: thy right hand hath upholden me.

These also that seek the hurt of my soul: they shall go under the earth.

Let them fall upon the edge of the sword: that they may be a portion for foxes.

But the king shall rejoice in God; all they also that swear by him shall be commended: for the mouth of them that speak lies shall be stopped.

Glory be, &c.

Ant. My soul thirsteth.

Chap. Wherefore, beloved, seeing that ye look for such things, be diligent that ye may be found of Him in peace, without spot and blameless.—2 *Pet.* iii. 14.

MONDAY.

Lord, have mercy upon us.
Christ, have mercy upon us.
Lord, have mercy upon us.

Our Father.

Let the Comforter, Which proceedeth from Thee, O Lord, enlighten our minds, we beseech Thee, and lead us, as Thy Son hath promised, into all truth; through the Same Thy Son Jesus Christ.

But, O my God, Thou knowest my great poverty and misery, and that of myself I can do nothing: Thou knowest how unworthy I am of this infinite favour; and Thou alone canst make me worthy. Oh! since Thou art so good as to invite me thus to Thyself, add this one bounty more to the rest, to prepare me for Thyself. Cleanse my soul from its stains, clothe it with the wedding-garment of charity, adorn it with all virtues, and make it a fit abode for Thee. Drive sin and the devil far from this dwelling, which Thou art here pleased to choose for Thyself, and make me well-pleasing in Thy sight: that this heavenly visit, which Thou deignest for my salvation, may not by my unworthiness be perverted to my damnation.

O Merciful Jesu, let that immortal Food, which in the holy Eucharist Thou vouchsafest me, instil into my weak and languishing soul new supplies of grace, new love, new vigour and resolution, that I may never more faint, or droop, or tire in my duty.

O Crucified Love, raise in me fresh ardours of love and consolation, that it may henceforth be the greatest torment I can endure ever to offend Thee; that it may be my greatest delight to please Thee.

God the Father, God the Son, God the Holy Ghost, be with me and with mine, now and at the hour of death. Amen.

TUESDAY.

THANKFUL REMEMBRANCE OF CHRIST'S DEATH.

And above all things ye must give most humble and hearty thanks to God, the Father, the Son, and the Holy Ghost, for the redemption of the world by the death and passion of our Saviour Christ, both God and man; who did humble Himself, even to the death upon the Cross, for us, miserable sinners, who lay in darkness and the shadow of death; that He might make us the children of God, and exalt us to everlasting life.

At Morning Prayer.

In the Name of the Father, and of the Son, and of the Holy Ghost. Amen.

℣. O Lord, open Thou my lips;

℟. And my mouth shall shew forth Thy praise.

℣. O God, make speed to save me;

℟. O Lord, make haste to help me.

HYMN.

O Thou, before the world began,
Ordained a sacrifice for man;
And by the Eternal Spirit made
An offering in the sinner's stead:
The true Melchizedek art Thou,
Pleading in heaven for sinners now.

Thy years, O God, can never fail,
Nor Thy blest work within the veil;
Thy Sacrifice is ever new,
Of legal types the substance true;
Thyself the Lamb for sinners slain,
Thy Priesthood doth unchanged remain.

O that our faith may never move,
But stand unshaken as Thy love!
'Sure evidence of things unseen,'
Now let it pass the years between,
And view Thee bleeding on the Tree,
Our Victim and our Priest to be.   Amen.

Ant. Thou hast heard me also from among the horns of the unicorns.

PSALM 22.   *Tu autem, Domine.*

Be not thou far from me, O Lord: thou art my succour, haste thee to help me.

Deliver my soul from the sword: my darling from the power of the dog.

Save me from the lion's mouth: thou hast heard me also from among the horns of the unicorns.

I will declare thy Name unto my brethren: in the midst of the congregation will I praise thee.

O praise the Lord, ye that fear him: magnify him, all ye of the seed of Jacob, and fear him, all ye seed of Israel;

For he hath not despised, nor abhorred, the low estate of the poor: he hath not hid his face from him, but when he called unto him he heard him.

My praise is of thee in the great congregation: my vows will I perform in the sight of them that fear him.

The poor shall eat, and be satisfied: they that seek after the Lord shall praise him; your heart shall live for ever.

TUESDAY.

All the ends of the world shall remember themselves, and be turned unto the Lord: and all the kindreds of the nations shall worship before him.

For the kingdom is the Lord's: and he is the Governour among the people.

All such as be fat upon earth: have eaten, and worshipped.

All they that go down into the dust shall kneel before him: and no man hath quickened his own soul.

My seed shall serve him: they shall be counted unto the Lord for a generation.

Glory be, &c.

Ant. Thou hast heard me.

Chap. But God commendeth His love towards us, in that, while we were yet sinners, Christ died for us. Much more then, being now justified by His blood, we shall be saved from wrath through Him.—*Rom.* v. 8, 9.

 Lord, have mercy upon us.
 Christ, have mercy upon us.
 Lord, have mercy upon us.
  Our Father.

O Lord Jesu Christ, Who out of the love of the Eternal Father, and seeking in and through all things, not Thine own but His glory, didst give up Thyself for us as an Offering and Sacrifice to God for a sweet-smelling savour; I praise and adore Thy supreme power, goodness, wisdom, justice, and mercy, which so wondrously shine forth in this Sacrifice and work of Redemption.

All glory, honour, and praise be to Thee, O Lord Jesu Christ; may all the world adore Thee: blessed be Thy holy Name, Who for us sinners didst vouchsafe to be born of a Virgin. Blessed be Thou, Who of Thine infinite goodness didst die on the Cross for our Redemption. Have mercy on us, most merciful Saviour, and so dispose our lives here by Thy grace, that we may hereafter rejoice with Thee in Thy glory. Amen.

For Thou hast compassion upon all things, O Lord, and hatest nothing that Thou hast made. Remember whereof we are made, for Thou art our Father, Thou art our God: be not angry very sore, and shut not up the multitude of Thy compassions upon us. For not in our own righteousness do we cast down our prayers before Thy Face, but in Thy manifold mercies. Take away from us all our iniquities, and mercifully kindle within us the fire of Thy Holy Spirit. Take away the heart of stone out of our flesh: and give us a heart of flesh, to love Thee, choose Thee alone, delight in Thee, follow Thee, enjoy Thee. We pray Thee, Lord, of Thy mercy, favourably regard this Thy family, which offer their service to Thy holy Name; and that the prayers of none may be void, no desire unheard, do Thou

TUESDAY.

teach us the prayers which Thou wilt be pleased favourably to hear and to grant.

O Mysterious God, ineffable and glorious Majesty, what is this that Thou hast done to the sons of men? Thou hast from Thy bosom sent Thy Son to take upon Him our nature; in Him Thou hast opened the fountains of Thy mercy. Admit me, O God, to this great effusion of loving-kindness, that I may partake of the Lord Jesus; that in Him I may be comforted in all my griefs, satisfied in all my doubts, healed of all my wounds; and being filled with the bread of Heaven, and armed with the strength of the Spirit, I may begin, continue, and end my journey unto the same place whither our Lord is gone before to prepare a mansion for each loving and obedient soul. Grant this, O Eternal God, for His sake Who died for us, Who intercedes for us, and gives Himself daily to us, our Lord and Saviour Jesus Christ. Amen.

God the Father, God the Son, God the Holy Ghost, be with me and with mine, now and at the hour of death. Amen.

BEFORE HOLY COMMUNION.

At Evening Prayer.

In the Name of the Father, and of the Son, and of the Holy Ghost. Amen.

℣. O Lord, open Thou my lips;

℟. And my mouth shall shew forth Thy praise.

℣. O God, make speed to save me;

℟. O Lord, make haste to help me.

Ant. He sent redemption unto His people, He hath commanded His covenant for ever.

PSALM 111. *Confitebor tibi.*

I will give thanks unto the Lord with my whole heart: secretly among the faithful, and in the congregation.

The works of the Lord are great: sought out of all them that have pleasure therein.

His work is worthy to be praised, and had in honour: and his righteousness endureth for ever.

The merciful and gracious Lord hath so done his marvellous works: that they ought to be had in remembrance.

He hath given meat unto them that fear him: he shall ever be mindful of his covenant.

He hath shewed his people the power of his works: that he may give them the heritage of the heathen.

The works of his hands are verity and judgement: all his commandments are true.

They stand fast for ever and ever: and are done in truth and equity.

He sent redemption unto his people: he hath commanded his covenant for ever; holy and reverend is his Name.

The fear of the Lord is the beginning of wisdom: a good understanding have all they that do thereafter; the praise of it endureth for ever.

Glory be, &c.

TUESDAY.

Ant. He sent redemption.

Chap. Christ being come an high priest of good things to come, by a greater and more perfect tabernacle, not made with hands, that is to say, not of this building; neither by the blood of goats and calves, but by His own blood He entered in once into the holy place, having obtained eternal redemption for us.— *Heb.* ix. 11, 12.

   Lord, have mercy upon us.
   Christ, have mercy upon us.
   Lord, have mercy upon us.
     Our Father.

O Heavenly Father, settle in my soul a lively faith in Thy mercy through Christ, a steady belief of all Thy love to sinners, and an affectionate reliance on the merits and mediation of Thy crucified Son, and on our being accepted in the Beloved, for Whom I will ever adore and love Thee.

Let the remembrance of Thy Death, O Lord Jesu, make me to desire and pant after Thee, that I may delight in Thy gracious presence; that with praise and thanksgiving, with jubilation and triumph, I may receive Thee into my heart.

That I may with a grateful heart meditate

on this work of such exceeding love, and commemorate it in this sacred Mystery,
> I beseech Thee to hear me, O Lord.

That His Body and Blood may not be unto me for judgment and condemnation, but for life and salvation,
> I beseech Thee to hear me, O Lord.

That I may never be ungrateful for the blessings of such Thine unspeakable grace and love,
> I beseech Thee to hear me, O Lord.

That through Him I may obtain from Thee pardon and forgiveness of all my sins; for, behold, He is the Lamb of God, That taketh away the sins of the world,
> I beseech Thee to hear me, O Lord.

And because of my own doings I am not able to please Thee, look upon the Face of Thy Christ, that through Him I may find grace in Thy sight. Have mercy upon me, that I may obtain this one thing, for which I earnestly pray, that I may never receive the Mysteries of the Body and Blood of Thy Son unworthily, or to my condemnation.

God the Father, God the Son, God the Holy Ghost, be with me and with mine, now and at the hour of death. Amen.

WEDNESDAY.

INTERCESSION.

Be in perfect charity with all men.

At Morning Prayer.

In the Name of the Father, and of the Son, and of the Holy Ghost. Amen.

℣. O Lord, open Thou my lips;

℟. And my mouth shall shew forth Thy praise.

℣. O God, make speed to save me;

℟. O Lord, make haste to help me.

HYMN.

Lord of our life, and God of our salvation,
Star of our night, and hope of every nation,
Hear and receive Thy Church's supplication,
        Lord God Almighty.

See round Thine ark the hungry billows curling,
See how Thy foes their banners are unfurling:
Lord, while their darts envenomed they are hurling,
        Thou canst preserve us.

BEFORE HOLY COMMUNION.

Lord, Thou canst help when earthly armour faileth;
Lord, Thou canst save when deadly sin assaileth;
Lord, o'er Thy Rock nor death nor hell prevaileth;
> Grant us Thy peace, Lord.

Peace in our hearts, our evil thoughts assuaging;
Peace in Thy Church, where brothers are engaging;
Peace, when the world its busy war is waging;
> Calm Thy foes' raging.

Grant us Thy help till backward they are driven;
Grant them Thy truth, that they may be forgiven;
Grant peace on earth, or, after we have striven,
> Peace in Thy Heaven. Amen.

Ant. For there the Lord promised His blessing, and life for evermore.

PSALM 133. *Ecce, quam bonum!*

Behold, how good and joyful a thing it is: brethren, to dwell together in unity!

It is like the precious ointment upon the head, that ran down unto the beard: even unto Aaron's beard, that went down to the skirts of his clothing.

Like as the dew of Hermon: which fell upon the hill of Sion.

For there the Lord promised his blessing: and life for evermore.

Glory be, &c.

WEDNESDAY.

Ant. For there the Lord.

Chap. Praying always with all prayer and supplication in the Spirit, and watching thereunto with all perseverance and supplication for all saints.—*Eph.* vi. 18.

> Lord, have mercy upon us.
> Christ, have mercy upon us.
> Lord, have mercy upon us.
>
> Our Father.

O Lord, Who hast taught us that all our doings without charity are nothing worth; send Thy Holy Ghost, and pour into our hearts that most excellent gift of charity, the very bond of peace and of all virtues, without which whosoever liveth is counted dead before Thee. Grant this for Thine only Son Jesus Christ's sake. Amen.

O God of infinite mercy, Who hast compassion on all men and relievest the necessities of all that call to Thee for help; hear the prayers of Thy servant who is unworthy to ask anything for himself, yet in humility and duty is bound to pray for others.

Almighty, everlasting God, we humbly beseech Thee to hear our prayers, and grant that we, whom Thou permittest to join in offering to Thee the Sacrifice of Thy Son, may by the virtue thereof obtain that which we desire.

For His sake look upon the Church His Spouse, which He purchased with His own Blood, that He might present her to Himself beautiful, without spot or wrinkle. Increase in her faith, hope, charity.

Break Thou the pride of her persecutors and enemies.

Root out heresies and schisms.

Pour the light of Thy truth upon such as are now aliens from the Faith, and bring them into Thy fold.

Let not so many souls perish, which have been formed after Thine Image, and redeemed by the Blood of Thy Son.

O Thou, Who walkest in the midst of the golden candlesticks,

Remove not our candlestick out of its place;

Set in order the things that are wanting;

Establish what remains and is ready to perish.

Lord of the harvest, send forth labourers into Thy harvest.

Have mercy on all, O Lord, and more especially hear me while I pray to Thee,

For our fathers in holy things, our Bishops,

WEDNESDAY.

(especially the Bishop of this diocese), all guides of souls, and all who wait at Thine altar;

That they being clothed with righteousness, may give their account with joy:

For our Queen, and for all Christian Kings, Princes, and Magistrates;

That Thou wouldest give them faithful care for their subjects, zeal and constancy in defence of the Faith and of Thy Church.

For our labourers and artisans;

For those that travel;

For the sick, especially —— ;

For the weary-hearted, the desolate, the widow, the orphan;

For the troubled in mind;

For those who are in any kind of temptation or special danger;

For my parents, godparents, and all in authority over me,

Rewarding sevenfold their goodness towards me;

For my brothers, my sisters, my godchildren;

For all to whom my soul has been knit, especially —— ;

For all my benefactors;

For all who have been kind to me;

For all whom I have hurt, wronged, or

tempted, knowingly or unknowingly; and for all who have used me ill:

On all these have mercy, O Lord;

Blessing them and helping them as Thou seest most fit;

To those who have departed in Thy faith and fear,

Grant, O Lord, eternal rest;

And may perpetual light shine on them.

Bless, O Lord, him to whom Thou hast given the spiritual care of me, Thy child. Grant that at the last day I may not be an occasion of grief or shame to him, but one of the jewels in the crown Thou wilt give him, and be with him admitted to see that blessed Face which here he hath taught me to love. Amen.

Lord, when I present myself and my love, as all the gift I have to offer at Thine altar, next to my love for Thee, and for the sake of Thine infinite love to me, which I there remember, give me grace to love my neighbour, and to be in charity with all men, and to walk in love, as Thou hast loved me. Amen.

For, O Lord, mindful of Thy venerable Passion, I approach to Thine altar to join in offering unto Thee that Sacrifice which Thou hast instituted and commanded to be offered in remembrance of Thee for our well-being. Receive it, we beseech Thee, O God most High, for Thy Holy Church, and for the people whom Thou hast purchased with Thy Blood. We bring before Thee, Lord, if Thou wilt graciously vouchsafe to behold, the tribulations of the people, the groans of prisoners, the miseries of orphans, the necessities of strangers; the helplessness of the weak, the depressions of the languishing, the infirmities of the aged, the aspirations of young men, the vows of virgins, the wailings of widows.

God the Father, God the Son, God the Holy Ghost, be with me and with mine, now and at the hour of death. Amen.

At Evening Prayer.

In the Name of the Father, and of the Son, and of the Holy Ghost. Amen.

℣. O Lord, open Thou my lips;

℟. And my mouth shall shew forth Thy praise.

℣. O God, make speed to save me;

℟. O Lord, make haste to help me.

Ant. O pray for the peace of Jerusalem.

BEFORE HOLY COMMUNION.

Psalm 122. *Lætatus sum.*

I was glad when they said unto me: We will go into the house of the Lord.

Our feet shall stand in thy gates: O Jerusalem.

Jerusalem is built as a city: that is at unity in itself.

For thither the tribes go up, even the tribes of the Lord: to testify unto Israel, to give thanks unto the Name of the Lord.

For there is the seat of judgement: even the seat of the house of David.

O pray for the peace of Jerusalem: they shall prosper that love thee.

Peace be within thy walls: and plenteousness within thy palaces.

For my brethren and companions' sakes: I will wish thee prosperity.

Yea, because of the house of the Lord our God: I will seek to do thee good.

Glory be, &c.

Ant. O pray.

Chap. Pray for one another, that ye may be healed. The effectual fervent prayer of a righteous man availeth much.—*S. James* v. 16.

Lord, have mercy upon us.
Christ, have mercy upon us.
Lord, have mercy upon us.
Our Father.

O God, Who willest not the death of a sinner, look with compassion upon those who do not know Thee. Have pity on all, that they may be converted and live. Avenge Thyself upon Thine enemies, by overwhelming them with Thy mercy; penetrate their hearts with a ray of Thy grace, that it may call forth in them feelings of true repentance, which may disarm Thine anger. Take iniquity from the

WEDNESDAY.

midst of us, restore to Thy holy religion the lustre and beauty of former days, extinguish hatred and revenge, make innocence and piety to flourish anew. May all men bless Thy holy name, and cherish Thy holy law; that sincere repentance and change of heart may obtain for them, of Thy goodness, the happiness of loving and praising Thee for all eternity, through Jesus Christ our Lord. Amen.

O Lord Jesu Christ, the spotless Lamb of God, Who lovest purity and undefiledness, remember not, we beseech Thee, our offences or the offences of our forefathers, but hear us who humbly pray that Thou wouldst have mercy upon all sinners. Cleanse, we beseech Thee, our cities from all impurity; keep the young from the seductions of worldly pleasure; restrain the headstrong passions of men: and of Thy tender compassion give repentance to all poor women who are living in open impurity, touching their hearts with Thy love; so that at last, they and all those who have encouraged them in sin may hear Thy precious words of forgiveness, and be received into Thy kingdom, Who livest and reignest with the Father and the Holy Ghost, ever one God, world without end. Amen.

Give perfection to beginners; give understanding to the little ones; give aid to those who are running their course. Give compunction to the negligent; give fervour of spirit to the lukewarm; give to the perfect a good consummation. Even so, Lord Jesus.

O Almighty and eternal God, Who hast dominion over the living and the dead, I humbly beseech Thee, that they for whom I have purposed to offer my prayers, whether this world still retain them in the flesh, or the next hath received them out of their bodies, may, by the clemency of Thy goodness, obtain pardon and full remission of all their sins, through our Lord Jesus Christ. Amen.

O Lord, hear my prayer;
And let my cry come unto Thee.

May the souls of the faithful, through the mercy of God, rest in peace. Amen.

THURSDAY.

COMMEMORATION OF THE INSTITUTION.

And to the end that we should always remember the exceeding great love of our Master, and only Saviour, Jesus Christ, thus dying for us, and the innumerable benefits which by His precious blood-shedding He hath obtained to us; He hath instituted and ordained holy mysteries, as pledges of His love, and for a continual remembrance of His death, to our great and endless comfort.

At Morning Prayer.

In the Name of the Father, and of the Son, and of the Holy Ghost.   Amen.

℣. Lamb of God, that takest away the sins of the world,

℟. Have mercy upon us.

HYMN.

According to Thy gracious word,
  In deep humility,
This will I do, my dying Lord ;
  I will remember Thee.

Thy Body, broken for my sake,
  My bread from Heaven shall be;
The cup, Thy precious Blood, I'll take,
  And thus remember Thee.

When to the Cross I turn mine eyes,
  And gaze on Calvary,
O Lamb of God, my Sacrifice,
  I must remember Thee;

Remember Thee, and all Thy pains,
  And all Thy love to me;
Yea, while a breath, a pulse remains,
  I will remember Thee.

And when these failing lips grow dumb,
  And mind and memory flee,
When Thou shalt in Thy kingdom come,
  Jesus, remember me!

To Thee, O Jesu, Light of Light,
  All praise and glory be;
To God the Father infinite,
  And, Holy Ghost, to Thee.   Amen.

Ant. He hath given meat unto them that fear Him; He shall ever be mindful of His covenant.

THURSDAY.

Psalm III. *Confitebor tibi.*

I will give thanks unto the Lord with my whole heart: secretly among the faithful, and in the congregation.

The works of the Lord are great: sought out of all them that have pleasure therein.

His work is worthy to be praised, and had in honour: and His righteousness endureth for ever.

The merciful and gracious Lord hath so done his marvellous works: that they ought to be had in remembrance.

He hath given meat unto them that fear him: he shall ever be mindful of his covenant.

He hath shewed his people the power of his works: that he may give them the heritage of the heathen.

The works of his hands are verity and judgement: all his commandments are true.

They stand fast for ever and ever: and are done in truth and equity.

He sent redemption unto his people: he hath commanded his covenant for ever; holy and reverend is his Name.

The fear of the Lord is the beginning of wisdom: a good understanding have all they that do thereafter; the praise of it endureth for ever.

Glory be, &c.

Ant. He hath given meat.

Chap. Christ our Passover is sacrificed for us: therefore let us keep the Feast, not with old leaven, neither with the leaven of malice and wickedness; but with the unleavened bread of sincerity and truth.—1 *Cor.* v. 7, 8.

Lord, have mercy upon us.
Christ, have mercy upon us.
Lord, have mercy upon us.

Our Father.

Eternal thanks be to Thee, O Thou Creator and Redeemer of men, Who, to manifest Thy love to the whole world, hast prepared a great Supper, wherein Thou hast given us for food, not the typical lamb of old, but Thy most sacred Body and Blood, rejoicing the faithful with Thy holy banquet, and replenishing them with the cup of Thy Salvation.

I pray Thee, O Lord, by this same all-holy mystery of Thy Body and Blood, whereby in Thy Church Thou feedest us and givest us to drink, washest and sanctifiest us, and makest us partakers of the one supreme Divine nature, grant me to be filled with all Thy holy graces, that I may, with a good conscience, approach Thine altar, so that these holy mysteries may be made to me salvation and life. For Thou hast said with Thy holy and blessed mouth, 'The bread which I will give is My Flesh, which I will give for the life of the world: I am the living bread which came down from heaven; if any man shall eat of this bread, he shall live for ever.'

O most sweet Bread, heal the palate of my heart, that I may taste the sweetness of Thy love. Heal it of all infirmities, that I may find sweetness in nothing out of Thee. O most pure

Bread, Who hast in Thyself all delight and all savour, Who ever refreshest us and never failest in Thyself, let my heart feed on Thee, and may my inmost soul be filled with the sweetness of Thy savour. The Angels feed on Thee fully; let pilgrim man feed on Thee after his measure, that he may never fail in the way, being refreshed with such food for the way.

Holy Bread, living Bread, pure Bread, Who camest down from Heaven, and givest life unto the world, come into my heart, and cleanse me from all defilement of flesh and spirit. Enter into my soul, heal and cleanse me within and without. Be the protection and continual health of my soul and body. Drive far from me those who lay wait for me. Let my enemies remove far away from the presence of Thy power; so that fenced within and without by Thee, I may, by a strait way, arrive at Thy kingdom, where, not as now, in mysteries, but face to face we shall behold Thee: when Thou shalt have delivered up the kingdom to God and the Father, and God shall be all in all. For then shalt Thou satisfy me with Thyself by a marvellous fulness, so that I shall neither hunger nor thirst any more; Who, with the same God the Father and Holy Spirit, livest and reignest throughout all ages. Amen.

O Christ, hear us.

O God the Father, of heaven,
O God the Son, Redeemer of the world,
O God the Holy Ghost,
Holy Trinity, one God,
} *Have mercy upon us.*

Be merciful, spare us, O Lord.

From the snares of the Devil,
From the peril of death,
From evil thoughts,
From hardness of heart,
By Thy pierced Side,
By Thy five Wounds,
By Thy Sacraments,
} *Good Lord, deliver us.*

We sinners beseech Thee to hear us:

That Thou wilt give us sure hope,
That Thou wilt grant us true faith,
That Thou wilt endue us with perfect charity,
That Thou wilt renew our souls and bodies by this most holy mystery,
That by it we may obtain pardon for all our sins,
That by it we may be able to cleave always to Thee,
That by it we may be worthy to dwell in Thee, and that Thou mayst dwell in us,
} *We beseech Thee to hear us, Good Lord.*

THURSDAY.

That Thou wilt vouchsafe to pour into our hearts the grace of Thy Holy Spirit,
That Thou wilt vouchsafe to preserve all Christian people, as Thou hast redeemed them by Thy precious Blood,
} We beseech Thee to hear us, Good Lord.

℣. O Lord, hear my prayer;
℟. And let my cry come unto Thee.

O God, Whose only Son ceased not to love His children unto the end; pour upon us the spirit of love, that we may worthily approach this mystery of His love, and follow the example of perfect humility which He has left us, to the end that being dead with Him Who died for us, we may rise again with Him to newness of life. Amen.

Grant also, O Good Jesu, that I may ever honour this awful mystery and wondrous gift with due faith, reverence, and gratitude, and receive it now and ever with a pure and glowing heart; may I give diligence to adorn the station to which Thou hast called me with charity, purity, humility, gentleness, patience, sobriety, and with all such behaviour as is pleasing to Thee, and becometh a faithful servant of Thine. Amen.

BEFORE HOLY COMMUNION.

O Lord Jesu Christ, Who hast vouchsafed to provide Thy Body and Blood for food and drink unto Thy servants, in the offering and reception whereof Thou willest to recal the memory of Thy Passion and Death ; give me grace that in performing this Thy most holy will, I may be able to receive the abundant fruits of this Sacrament.   Amen.

God the Father, God the Son, God the Holy Ghost, be with me and with mine, now and at the hour of death.   Amen.

At Evening Prayer.

In the Name of the Father, and of the Son, and of the Holy Ghost.   Amen.

Lamb of God, that takest away the sins of the world, have mercy upon us.

Ant. The eyes of all wait upon Thee, O Lord, and Thou givest them their meat in due season.

THURSDAY.

PSALM 145. *Exaltabo te, Deus.*

I will magnify thee, O God, my King, and I will praise thy Name for ever and ever.

Every day will I give thanks unto thee: and praise thy Name for ever and ever.

Great is the Lord, and marvellous, worthy to be praised: there is no end of his greatness.

One generation shall praise thy works unto another: and declare thy power.

As for me, I will be talking of thy worship: thy glory, thy praise, and wondrous works;

So that men shall speak of the might of thy marvellous acts: and I will also tell of thy greatness.

The memorial of thine abundant kindness shall be showed: and men shall sing of thy righteousness.

The Lord is gracious, and merciful: long-suffering, and of great goodness.

The Lord is loving unto every man: and his mercy is over all his works.

All thy works praise thee, O Lord: and thy saints give thanks unto thee.

They show the glory of thy kingdom: and talk of thy power;

That thy power, thy glory, and mightiness of thy kingdom: might be known unto men.

Thy kingdom is an everlasting kingdom: and thy dominion endureth throughout all ages.

The Lord upholdeth all such as fall: and lifteth up all those that are down.

The eyes of all wait upon thee, O Lord: and thou givest them their meat in due season.

Thou openest thine hand: and fillest things living with plenteousness.

Glory be, &c.

Ant. The eyes of all wait.

Chap. For it is not possible that the blood of bulls and of goats should take away sins. Wherefore, when He cometh into the world He saith, Sacrifice and offering Thou wouldest not, but a body hast Thou prepared Me.—*Heb.* x. 4, 5.

BEFORE HOLY COMMUNION.

Lord, have mercy upon us.
Christ, have mercy upon us.
Lord, have mercy upon us.
Our Father.

O God the Father, of Heaven,
O God the Son, Redeemer of the world,
O God the Holy Ghost,
O Holy Trinity, one God,
O Father, Who hast given us Thine only-begotten Son, the true Bread from Heaven,
O blessed Jesus, Who camest down to give life to the world,
O Holy Spirit, bond of the mystical union between Christ and His members,
} *Have mercy upon us.*

From receiving this holy Sacrament unworthily and to our condemnation :
From all neglect in coming to Thy holy table, and from all irreverence and negligence when we draw near to Thee :
From hungering and thirsting after earthly things, from all sin, and from everlasting death :
By that great love wherewith Thou didst institute this holy Sacrament ; by Thy Body broken on the Cross and bestowed on all who come in faith and love to this Sacrament :
} *Good Lord, deliver us.*

THURSDAY.

That our faith in Thee may never waver, our hope never fail, and our charity never decay:

That we may with all thankfulness commemorate Thy Passion in this blessed Sacrament, that our faith may be strengthened and our devotion quickened:

That by true repentance we may be brought to a more frequent reception thereof, so that at length, as the hart desireth the waterbrooks, our souls may long after Thee, the living God:

That Thou wilt wash us thoroughly from the guilt of our sins, that we may approach Thy table with joy and gladness:

That we may receive Thee into our hearts with love and fear, and thereby obtain pardon and forgiveness of all our sins:

That in this holy Sacrament we may so discern the Lord's Body and Blood, that it may not be to us judgment and condemnation, but life and salvation, and that worthily receiving the same we neither hunger nor thirst any more, nor die eternally:

That through the worthy participation thereof Thou mayst for ever abide in

We sinners beseech Thee to hear us.

BEFORE HOLY COMMUNION.

us, and we in Thee, and that as many as eat of this bread may be made one in Thy peace and love :

That in innocency we may compass Thine altar, O Lord, and offer up ourselves a living, holy, and acceptable sacrifice to Thee, and continue in Thy faith and fear unto our lives' end, and at length behold Thee, O Saviour, with open face in everlasting glory : } We sinners beseech Thee to hear us.

℣. Thou hast given us, O Lord, bread from Heaven ;
℟. Replenished with all sweetness and delight.
℣. Lord, hear our prayer ;
℟. And let our cry come unto Thee.

O God, Who in this wonderful Sacrament hast left us a perpetual memorial of Thy Passion ; grant us, we beseech Thee, so to reverence the sacred mysteries of Thy Body and Blood, that we may continually perceive in our souls the fruit of Thy redemption ; Who, with the Father and the Holy Ghost, livest and reignest ever one God, world without end. Amen.

O Lord, we beseech Thee, visit and cleanse

THURSDAY.

our consciences, that Thy Son our Lord Jesus Christ may when He cometh find in us a dwellingplace prepared for Him, Who liveth and reigneth with Thee in the unity of the Holy Ghost, ever one God, world without end.

God the Father, God the Son, God the Holy Ghost, be with me and with mine, now and at the hour of death. Amen.

FRIDAY.

HUMILIATION FOR SIN.

Ye that mind to come to the Holy Communion of the Body and Blood of our Saviour Christ, must consider how St. Paul exhorteth all persons diligently to try and examine themselves, before they presume to eat of that Bread and drink of that Cup. Judge therefore yourselves, brethren, that ye be not judged of the Lord; repent you truly for your sins past.

At Morning Prayer.

In the Name of the Father, and of the Son, and of the Holy Ghost. Amen.

Lamb of God, that takest away the sins of the world, have mercy upon us.

HYMN.

Saviour, when in dust to Thee
Low we bend the adoring knee;
When repentant to the skies
Scarce we lift our streaming eyes;
O by all the pains and woe
Suffered once for man below,
Bending from Thy throne on high,
Hear our solemn litany!

FRIDAY.

By Thine hour of agony;
By Thy prayer, thrice heard on high;
By Thy purple robe of scorn;
By Thy wounds, Thy crown of thorn;
By Thy cross, Thy pangs and cries;
By Thy perfect sacrifice—
Jesus, look with pitying eye,
Hear our solemn litany!

By Thy deep expiring groan;
By the sealed sepulchral stone;
By Thy triumph o'er the grave;
By Thy power from death to save;
Mighty God, ascended Lord,
To Thy throne in heaven restored—
Prince and Saviour, hear the cry
Of our solemn litany! Amen.

Ant. For innumerable troubles are come about me; my sins have taken such hold upon me that I am not able to look up: yea, they are more in number than the hairs of my head, and my heart hath failed me.

PSALM 38. *Iniquitates meæ.*

My wickednesses are gone over my head: and are like a sore burden, too heavy for me to bear.

My wounds stink, and are corrupt: through my foolishness.

I am brought into so great trouble and misery: that I go mourning all the day long.

For my loins are filled with a sore disease: and there is no whole part in my body.

I am feeble, and sore

smitten: I have roared for the very disquietness of my heart.

Lord, thou knowest all my desire: and my groaning is not hid from thee.

My heart panteth, my strength hath failed me: and the sight of mine eyes is gone from me.

My lovers and my neighbours did stand looking upon my trouble: and my kinsmen stood afar off.

They also that sought after my life laid snares for me: and they that went about to do me evil talked of wickedness, and imagined deceit all the day long.

As for me, I was like a deaf man, and heard not: and as one that is dumb, who doth not open his mouth.

I became even as a man that heareth not: and in whose mouth are no reproofs.

For in thee, O Lord, have I put my trust: thou shalt answer for me, O Lord my God.

I have required that they, even mine enemies, should not triumph over me: for when my foot slipped, they rejoiced greatly against me.

Glory be, &c.

Ant. For innumerable.

Chap. For He hath made Him to be sin for us, Who knew no sin; that we might be made the righteousness of God in Him.— 2 Cor. v. 21.

    Lord, have mercy upon us.
    Christ, have mercy upon us.
    Lord, have mercy upon us.
    Our Father.

O Christ, hear us.

O God the Father, of Heaven,
  O God the Son, Redeemer of the world,
O God the Holy Ghost,
O Holy Trinity, one God,

} Have mercy upon us.

FRIDAY.

Be gracious, spare us, O Lord.

From all evil,
From all sin,
From a sudden and wicked death,
By Thy toils and griefs,
By Thy blood shed for the remission of our sins,

} *Good Lord, deliver us.*

That it may please Thee to bring us to true repentance:
That condemning ourselves we may escape Thy condemnation:
That we may bring forth worthy fruits of repentance:
That we may yield our members servants to righteousness unto holiness:
That we may chasten our bodies, and bring them into subjection:
That sin may not reign in our mortal body:
That it may please Thee to purge us here, though it may be as by fire, and to spare us in eternity:

} *We beseech Thee to hear us, O Lord.*

℣. O Lord, deal not with us after our sins;

℟. Neither reward us after our iniquities.

℣. O Lord, remember not our old sins;

℟. Have mercy upon us soon, for we are brought very low.

℣. O Lord, cleanse Thou me from my secret faults;

℟. Keep Thy servant also from presumptuous sins.

℣. O Lord, turn Thy face from my sins;

℟. And put out all my misdeeds.

℣. O give me the comfort of Thy help again;

℟. And stablish me with Thy free Spirit.

℣. O Lord, hear my prayer;

℟. And let my cry come unto Thee.

O God, Who rejectest not the greatest sinner, but in loving pity art reconciled to him by penitence, mercifully regard our lowly supplications, and give us strength to fulfil Thy Commandments. Amen.

O Lord Christ, Whose will is by Thy sufferings to heal mine, and by Thy wounds to bind up the wounds of Thy servants, grant to me that have so often sinned against Thee tears of contrition and of repentance. Raise up to Thyself my mind which has been dragged down to the earth, and draw me out of the gulf of destruction: for I neither repent nor feel sorry as I ought for my sins, over which I cannot weep. My mind has become dull and darkened, and I have not power to look up to Thee when I am in trouble, neither can I be warmed by tears of love for Thee. But Thou, my Lord and Master, Thou treasure of all good, give me a deep sincere repentance and a heart earnest and intent on seeking Thee. Renew within me the features of Thine own image. I had forsaken Thee, but do not Thou forsake me; come forth to seek me and bring me back to Thy fold: make me a sheep of Thy chosen flock, and feed me with them in the green pastures of Thy Divine mysteries, O Jesus, my Lord and my God. Amen.

King of virgins, Who lovest purity and undefiledness, extinguish in me by the heavenly dew of Thy blessing whatsoever may kindle evil desire, that so purity of mind and body may abide in me. Mortify in my members every hurtful emotion, and give me true and persevering chastity with Thy other gifts which please Thee in truth, that so I may with chaste body and pure heart join in offering to Thee the sacrifice of praise. For with what mighty contrition of heart and fountain of tears, with what reverence and awe, with what purity of mind and body, should that Divine and Heavenly Sacrifice be celebrated, wherein Thy Flesh is indeed taken, and Thy Blood is indeed drunk; wherein things lowest and highest, earthly and Divine, are united, where is the presence of the holy Angels, where Thou art, in a wonderful and unspeakable way, both Sacrifice and Priest!

Who can worthily celebrate this Sacrament, unless Thou, O God Almighty, make him worthy? I know, O Lord, yea, truly do I know, and this do I confess to Thy loving mercy, that I am not worthy to approach so high a mystery, by reason of my many sins and numberless negligences. But I know, and truly do believe with my whole heart, and confess with my lips, that Thou canst make me worthy, Who alone canst make that clean which cometh out of an unclean, and make sinners to be righteous and holy. By this Thine Almighty power, I beseech Thee, grant to me, a sinner, to approach this holy Sacrifice with fear and trembling, with purity of heart and streams of tears, with spiritual gladness and heavenly joy. May my mind feel the sweetness of Thy most blessed presence, and the guardianship of Thy holy Angels round about me. Amen.

God the Father, God the Son, God the Holy Ghost, be with me and with mine, now and at the hour of death. Amen.

FRIDAY.

SELF-EXAMINATION.

The way and means thereto is: first, to examine your lives and conversations by the rule of God's commandments; and whereinsoever ye shall perceive yourselves to have offended, either by will, word, or deed, there to bewail your own sinfulness, and to confess yourselves to Almighty God, with full purpose of amendment of life. . . . And because it is requisite that no man should come to the holy Communion, but with a full trust in God's mercy, and with a quiet conscience; therefore if there be any of you, who by this means cannot quiet his own conscience herein, but requireth further comfort or counsel, let him come to me, or to some other discreet and learned minister of God's Word, and open his grief; that by the ministry of God's holy Word, he may receive the benefit of absolution, together with ghostly counsel and advice, to the quieting of his conscience, and avoiding of all scruple and doubtfulness.

O Lord God, Who lightenest every man that cometh into the world, let the light of Thy grace shine into my heart, that I may fully know my shortcomings and my sins, and may confess them with that true sorrow and contrition of heart which befits me before Thee, and may amend them to Thy honour and glory

and to the salvation of my soul, through Jesus Christ our Lord.   Amen.
Our Father.

FIRST COMMANDMENT [a].

Being less ashamed of sinning before God than of confessing our sin; repeating a sin, from the feeling that it would be as easy to confess a frequent as a solitary fault; giving our first waking thoughts to anything but God; neglecting to make our peace with Him in the evening, but presuming on the expectation of another day; giving way to repining; feeling as though He were dealing more hardly with us than with others; resisting or not yielding readily to the good thoughts He sends; neglecting to offer our actions to Him; doing and saying things *merely* in order to be praised, or to please ourselves, with no consideration of right and wrong; allowing our hearts in self-

---

[a] The following suggestions may perhaps be found useful by recalling some of those sins which are easily unnoticed or forgotten. It may be remembered that any outward helps to self-examination must always be very slight and imperfect; and that (in the words of one much revered) "every one really in earnest will virtually have a set of questions for his own particular use."

The more open and gross breaches of God's law are not here set down, being plainly mentioned in the words of each commandment.

FRIDAY.

praise, especially in comparison with others; depending on our own goodness, cleverness, amiability, &c. ; lukewarm in His work ; soon weary of it; not pleased at others surpassing us in it; consciously keeping back something instead of sacrificing all to Him ; allowing our minds to dwell on the troubles and difficulties of our life, rather than on its blessings, and thereby nourishing an unthankful spirit ; omitting prayers or other religious exercises ; not endeavouring earnestly to perform them rightly ; not asking for help to do so ; vain, proud of anything belonging to us ; speaking much of ourselves or our family, especially to gain praise; obstinate, impatient of what humbles us ; unwilling to be less considered than others.

SECOND COMMANDMENT.

Not submitting our judgment entirely to that of the Church ; allowing our minds to dwell on the false opinions held by others ; reading the writings of those not sound in the faith ; allowing the outward circumstances of public worship, the individual priest, the building, the music, the behaviour of the congregation, to hinder our earnest and devout attention to the service ; concealing or slurring over anything we believe out of regard to man in word or

BEFORE HOLY COMMUNION.

deed; neglecting to refer all to Christ as our Mediator, and to take all from Him as personally present; not trying to realise God's omnipresence, especially at times of prayer; making an idol of any person; thinking more of his affection, help, protection, &c., than of God's; too inconsolable at losing them; making an idol of money, by allowing it to engross our thoughts and occupy too much our time; by discontent at losing it; or otherwise.

THIRD COMMANDMENT.

Using any expression whose original meaning related to the Holy Name; not refraining from a jest when it relates to holy things or words; quoting the Bible with reference to worldly matters; giving way to careless or wilful wandering in prayer in Church; speaking on religious subjects without trying to feel them; not trying to feel reverent in Church; not honouring God's priests in word and in thought; being less outwardly reverent when alone than with others; telling a lie; exaggerating; not taking pains to be exactly accurate in relating things; making a show of more religion than we have; allowing it to be supposed that we use more religious exercises, are living in a holier state, &c., than we are; doing things to be seen of men; dealing deceitfully with our own

FRIDAY. 51

heart; not seriously calling ourselves to account how we have kept our Baptismal, our Confirmation, our Eucharistical, or other vows; behaving so as to make the Holy Name which we bear blasphemed.

FOURTH COMMANDMENT.

Neglecting due preparation and confession before Holy Communion; not confessing to man if necessary, but omitting such confession because disliked; when practised, not performing it to the best of our ability; not as earnest in seeking opportunities of receiving the Holy Communion as we should be in seeking our daily food; not going to Church, especially on Sundays and holydays; neglecting to keep Sunday holy, and as a day unlike other days; reading books, newspapers, &c., unfit for the day, or doing anything about which we have a scruple; making no difference in our thoughts and conversation between it and other days; not observing festivals and fasts in some real way; not giving our whole time to God, and, to this end, keeping some account of it; not doing on the week-days all that we have to do, as to Him; and on Sunday also, according to the difference; neglecting to cultivate our talents; being slothful in body or mind; not doing things at the right time; wasting time in idleness, or making others waste it; not thinking enough of our Christian privileges.

FIFTH COMMANDMENT.

Failing in love, honour, obedience, consideration, gratitude to parents or those in their place; speaking of them without due respect; neglecting to obey him who has the care of our souls; not honouring all clergy; not loving and honouring the Queen and Royal Family; repeating stories to their discredit; not paying due respect to old people, and to those in higher station than ourselves; neglecting to care for the souls and bodies of our children, servants, tenants, work-people, &c.; neglecting to pray for all these, also for our godchildren.

SIXTH COMMANDMENT.

Wanting in love to husband or wife, brothers and sisters, or other near relations; not bearing with their faults and making allowance for them; forgetting that all Christians are members of Christ, and not treating them as such; being angry without sufficient cause; taking offence; easily provoked; being sullen; bearing malice; wishing for vexations to others, or not sorry for them; thinking evil of others; giving way to impatience at others' stupidity,

FRIDAY.

and speaking hastily; being put out at not having our own way; neglecting to give sympathy, or not caring whether we receive it; nourishing jealousy, or personal dislike or prejudice; provoking or in any way tempting others to sin, or not watching lest we do so; not telling them of their faults when it is clearly our duty, or speaking more severely than is needful; not as glad for others' good as our own; neglecting our own or others' health.

SEVENTH COMMANDMENT.

Allowing ourselves to look at, or listen to, or draw near to, or imagine anything which occasions thoughts of which we should be ashamed if known; giving way to such thoughts; being selfish in our pleasures; not keeping rules in diet, dress, sleep, &c.; thinking much of bodily comfort; grudging trouble, &c., that interferes with it; lying down, using easy chairs, &c., more than is needful; being slothful and unwilling to give ourselves trouble; caring too much to have things about us in the best taste, of the best materials, &c.; complaining of the food provided for us.

EIGHTH COMMANDMENT.

Careless about money; spending too much in trifles; not giving at least a tenth directly to God and His poor; careless about repaying what we have borrowed; not being *ready* to give and *glad* to distribute; being unwilling to lend to others; not taking care of what is lent to us; prying into things we have no right to know; interfering in other people's affairs; not being careful to give others the full amount of credit, honour, consideration due to them; grudging what we give or rightly spend.

NINTH COMMANDMENT.

Repeating evil of others without knowing it to be true, or, if so knowing it, without necessity; misrepresenting anything said, or not being careful to repeat it quite accurately; putting a bad interpretation on others' words or deeds; not being sorry to hear ill of another; telling any secret; repeating to any one what a third person has said of him; flattering others; praising them falsely, out of good nature; misleading others as to the character of a servant, or other person employed, out of good nature.

TENTH COMMANDMENT.

Not trying to put down the first thought of sin; not trying to put away the desire for what God has withheld; being annoyed at the sight of bodily, mental, or outward gifts in

FRIDAY.

others which we do not possess; desiring to engross the applause or good opinion of others; being discontented with, or too much lifted up by, our own share of things; not making God's will, and not our own pleasure, our rule of life.

Almighty and everlasting God, who hatest nothing that Thou hast made, and dost forgive the sins of all them that are penitent; create and make in us new and contrite hearts, that we worthily lamenting our sins, and acknowledging our wretchedness, may obtain of Thee, the God of all mercy, perfect remission and forgiveness; through Jesus Christ our Lord. Amen.

O Lord Jesu Christ, Very God and Very Man, my Creator and Redeemer; I grieve with my whole heart that I have offended Thee, my Lord and my God; Whom I desire to love above all things: I accuse myself of the wrong desires and thoughts which I have conceived, especially . . . . . ; of the unholy words which I have spoken, especially . . . . ; of the sinful and ungodly deeds which I have committed, especially . . . . . : I desire earnestly to sin no more, and to shun all occasions of sin. And in satisfaction for my sins, I offer to Thee Thy most sacred life, Thy Passion and Thy Death, and the whole price of Thy Blood, which was shed for us. And I trust that of Thine infinite goodness and mercy, Thou wilt, by the merits of Thy precious Blood, forgive me all my sins; and that Thou wilt pour on me the riches of Thy grace, whereby I may live holily and serve Thee perfectly to the end; Who with the Father and the Holy Ghost livest and reignest, God Blessed for ever. Amen.

>Lord, have mercy upon us.
>Christ, have mercy upon us.
>Lord, have mercy upon us.
>Our Father.

Maker of heaven and earth, King of kings, and Lord of lords, Who hast made me out of nothing in Thine image and likeness, and hast redeemed me with Thine own Blood; sinner that I am, I am not worthy to name Thee, to call on Thee, to think on Thee in my heart. I humbly pray Thee, I meekly entreat Thee, look on me, Thy wicked servant, in mercy. Have mercy on me, Thou Who hadst mercy on the woman of Canaan and Mary Magdalene, Thou that sparedst the publican, and the thief upon the cross. I confess my sins to Thee, most merciful Father; if I wished to hide them, I could not from Thee, Lord. Spare me, O Christ, Whom I have so late and so much offended by thought, word, and deed ; yea, in whatsoever way I could possibly sin against Thee, by my fault, by my own fault, by my most grievous fault, poor miserable sinner. Wherefore, Lord, I pray Thy pity, Who didst come down from Heaven to save me. Thou raisedst David from his fall, spare me, O Lord ; O Christ, spare me, Who sparedst Peter when he had denied Thee. Thou art my Creator and Redeemer, my King and my God. Thou art my Hope and my Trust ; my Comfort and my Strength ; my Defence and my Deliverance ; my Life, my Health, and my Resurrection ; my Help and my Protection. I pray and entreat Thee help me, and I shall be safe ; direct me and defend me ; strengthen me and comfort me ; enlighten me and come unto me. Raise me from the dead : Lord, despise me not ; I am Thy servant, vile though I be, worthless, and a sinner. Such as I am, good or bad, I am Thine. Own me as Thine own, who fly to Thee for refuge ; though I be worthless and unclean, Thou canst cleanse me ; though blind, Thou canst enlighten me ; though sick, Thou canst heal me; yea, though dead and buried, Thou canst raise me up; Thy mercy is more than my iniquity; Thy pity than my impiety; Thou canst remit more than I commit; Thou canst spare more than I can err. Despise me not then, O Lord; neither regard the multitude of my iniquities; but according to the multitude of Thy mercies have mercy upon me, and be gracious to me, the chief of sinners. Say unto my soul, I am Thy salvation, O Thou who hast said, I desire not the death of a sinner, but rather that he should be converted and live. Turn Thee unto me, O Lord, and be not angry against me. I implore Thee, most pitiful Father, I pray Thee meekly of Thy great mercy, bring me to a holy end, and to true penitence for all my sins. Amen.

PSALM 51. *Miserere mei, Deus.*

Have mercy upon me, O God, after thy great goodness: according to the multitude of thy mercies do away mine offences.

Wash me throughly from my wickedness: and cleanse me from my sin.

For I acknowledge my faults: and my sin is ever before me.

Against thee only have I sinned, and done this evil in thy sight: that thou mightest be justified in thy saying, and clear when thou art judged.

Behold, I was shapen in wickedness: and in sin hath my mother conceived me.

But lo, thou requirest truth in the inward parts: and shalt make me to understand wisdom secretly.

Thou shalt purge me with hyssop, and I shall be clean: thou shalt wash me, and I shall be whiter than snow.

Thou shalt make me hear of joy and gladness: that the bones which thou hast broken may rejoice.

Turn thy face from my sins: and put out all my misdeeds.

Make me a clean heart, O God: and renew a right spirit within me.

Cast me not away from thy presence: and take not thy holy Spirit from me.

O give me the comfort of thy help again: and stablish me with thy free Spirit.

Then shall I teach thy ways unto the wicked: and sinners shall be converted unto thee.

Deliver me from blood-guiltiness, O God, thou that art the God of my health: and my tongue shall sing of thy righteousness.

Thou shalt open my lips, O Lord: and my mouth shall shew thy praise.

For thou desirest no sacrifice, else would I give it thee: but thou delightest not in burnt-offerings.

The sacrifice of God is a troubled spirit: a broken and contrite heart, O God, shalt thou not despise.

O be favourable and gracious unto Sion: build thou the walls of Jerusalem.

Then shalt thou be pleased with the sacrifice of righteousness, with the burnt-offerings and oblations: then shall they offer young bullocks upon thine altar.

Glory be, &c.

At Evening Prayer.

In the Name of the Father, and of the Son, and of the Holy Ghost. Amen.

Lamb of God, that takest away the sins of the world, have mercy upon us.

Ant. Enter not into judgment with Thy servant.

BEFORE HOLY COMMUNION.

Psalm 143. *Domine, exaudi.*

Hear my prayer, O Lord, and consider my desire: hearken unto me for thy truth and righteousness' sake.

And enter not into judgement with thy servant: for in thy sight shall no man living be justified.

For the enemy hath persecuted my soul; he hath smitten my life down to the ground: he hath laid me in the darkness, as the men that have been long dead.

Therefore is my spirit vexed within me: and my heart within me is desolate.

Yet do I remember the time past; I muse upon all thy works: yea, I exercise myself in the works of thy hands.

I stretch forth my hands unto thee: my soul gaspeth unto thee as a thirsty land.

Hear me, O Lord, and that soon, for my spirit waxeth faint: hide not thy face from me, lest I be like unto them that go down into the pit.

O let me hear thy loving-kindness betimes in the morning, for in thee is my trust: shew thou me the way that I should walk in, for I lift up my soul unto thee.

Deliver me, O Lord, from mine enemies: for I flee unto thee to hide me.

Teach me to do the thing that pleaseth thee, for thou art my God: let thy loving Spirit lead me forth into the land of righteousness.

Quicken me, O Lord, for thy Name's sake: and for thy righteousness' sake bring my soul out of trouble.

And of thy goodness slay mine enemies: and destroy all them that vex my soul: for I am thy servant.

Glory be, &c.

Ant. Enter not.

Chap. Let us draw near with a true heart, in full assurance of faith, having our hearts sprinkled from an evil conscience, and our bodies washed with pure water.—*Heb.* x. 22.

FRIDAY.

Lord, have mercy upon us.
Christ, have mercy upon us.
Lord, have mercy upon us.

Our Father.

O Father of immeasurable goodness, if Thou shouldest mark our sins and wickednesses, who shall stand? So grievously in many things do we offend all. I pray Thee, therefore, of Thine everlasting love, forgive me my sins, wheresoever, whensoever, howsoever committed; forgive me if, at any time, I have not satisfied Thy commandment in wholly forgiving others, or if I have not loved my enemies from my heart. Amen.

O most sweet Lord Jesus Christ, I, unworthy sinner, call to Thy memory all the holy thoughts which from eternity hitherto Thou hast ever had, above all that one, whereby Thou, eternal Word, thoughtest to become man. O most merciful Lord, I pray from my heart of hearts that Thou in turn wilt pardon me all the vain, foul, and evil thoughts which, up to this time, I have entertained, or in any way caused others to entertain. O most piteous Lord Jesu Christ, I, miserable sinner, call to Thy memory all the good and health-giving words which Thou ever utteredst on earth. I pray Thee humbly, O good Jesu, forgive me all the words which up to this time I have uttered against Thy will, or caused others to utter. O most sweet Jesu Christ, I, unworthy sinner, yet redeemed by Thy precious Blood, call to Thy memory all the good works which, for our salvation, Thou wroughtest in the earth. I beseech Thee, most piteous Lord, pardon me whatsoever, by my ill-doing, I have, knowingly or unknowingly, committed against Thy law, and the glory of Thy Name, or have caused others to commit. And now, O most kind Lord, direct and order all my thoughts, words, and works, according to Thy good pleasure, to the praise of Thy Name; and conform them to the perfect rule of Thy most holy life and conversation. Thine I am, O Lord, and will be, in life and in death; into Thy hands I commend myself, and all that I am.

Purge me with the hyssop of Thy Blood, and I shall be clean. Wash me, and I shall be whiter than snow.

O Jesu, Saviour of the world, Who camest to save sinners, and saidst, Come unto Me, all ye that labour and are heavy laden, and I will refresh you; lo, I a sinner dare to come unto Thee, for with Thee there is plenteous redemption. I come unto Thee, from Whom I have erred and strayed as a sheep that is lost; but

FRIDAY.

O Thou Good Shepherd, Who didst lay down Thy life for Thy sheep, Who camest to seek and to save that which was lost, seek Thy servant, O Lord, for I do not forget Thy commandments. I come unto Thee, pierced with many wounds, grievously oppressed with so many evil passions; but Lord, if Thou wilt, Thou canst make me whole. Thou knowest that it is the sick who need a physician. But Thou art that Samaritan, the true Physician of souls, Who hast borne our griefs: Thou art He who gavest for the medicine for my soul the Sacrament of Thy precious Body and Blood. Have mercy therefore upon me, O Lord, and heal my soul, for I have sinned against Thee. A troubled spirit is a sacrifice unto Thee, O Lord; a broken and a contrite heart wilt Thou not despise. This do I desire to offer unto Thee, that I may the more safely join in offering the Sacrifice of Thy precious Body and Blood.

Break Thou therefore the bonds of my sins. For thus shall I worthily offer to Thee the sacrifice of praise and call upon the name of the Lord. Amen.

God the Father, God the Son, God the Holy Ghost, be with me and with mine, now and at the hour of death. Amen.

They will go from strength to strength: and unto the God of gods appeareth every one of them in Sion.

O Lord God of hosts, hear my prayer: hearken, O God of Jacob.

Behold, O God our defender: and look upon the face of thine Anointed.

For one day in thy courts: is better than a thousand.

I had rather be a doorkeeper in the house of my God: than to dwell in the tents of ungodliness.

For the Lord God is a light and defence: the Lord will give grace and worship, and no good thing shall be withhold from them that live a godly life.

O Lord God of hosts: blessed is the man that putteth his trust in thee.

Glory be, &c.

Ant. They will go.

Chap. I beseech you therefore, brethren, by the mercies of God, that ye present your bodies a living sacrifice, holy, acceptable unto God, which is your reasonable service. And be not conformed to this world; but be ye transformed by the renewing of your mind, that ye may prove what is that good, and acceptable, and perfect will of God.—*Rom.* xii. 1, 2.

    Lord, have mercy upon us.
    Christ, have mercy upon us.
    Lord, have mercy upon us.
    Our Father.

O God, the strength of all them that put their trust in Thee, mercifully accept our prayers; and because through the weakness of our mortal nature we can do no good thing

SATURDAY.

without Thee, grant us the help of Thy grace, that in keeping Thy commandments we may please Thee, both in will and deed; through Jesus Christ our Lord. Amen.

Lord, I am not worthy that Thou shouldest come under my roof, yet remember that Thou, being Lord of all, didst take upon Thee the form of a servant, and wast the friend of publicans and sinners. Let that humiliation of Thine, I pray Thee, move Thee not to despise me, vile and low as I am, but do Thou mercifully come unto me, or graciously receive me coming unto Thee.

O that my ways were made so direct that I might keep Thy statutes. But, O Lord, what will it profit me to will those things, unless Thou give power to perform them? Arise Thou therefore and help me, and give me strength, that the good which I will I may bring to good effect, that by the guidance of Thy grace I may so walk before Thee, that with all who are departed this life in Thy faith and fear, I may live with Thee and rejoice in Thee, and praise Thee throughout eternity.

O Blessed Lord, kindle such a holy flame in my heart that it may consume all my sins and vile affections, that I may never again defile the place which Thou hast chosen for Thy temple. Give me time and space to repent, and give me grace that as by Thy holy inspiration I do sincerely and stedfastly resolve on an entire reformation, so by Thy merciful guidance I may perform the same. Amen.

O Gracious Lord Jesu Christ, I Thy sinful servant, nothing presuming on my own deserts, but trusting in Thy mercy and goodness, with fear and trembling approach to the table of Thy most sweet feast. For my heart and body are defiled with many sins, my mind and tongue have not been faithfully guarded. So then, O gracious God, O terrible Majesty, I, miserable that I am, being in a great strait, turn to Thee, the fountain of mercy; to Thee I hasten to be cured; under Thy protection I flee; and I long to have Thee as my Saviour, before Whom I cannot stand as my Judge. To Thee, O Lord, I shew my wounds, to Thee I lay bare my shame. I know my sins, many and great, for which I fear. I hope in Thy mercies, which are countless. Look down, then, on me with the eyes of Thy mercy, O Lord Jesu Christ, Eternal King, God and man, crucified for man; hear me, who hope in Thee, have pity on me who am full of miseries and sins, Thou

SATURDAY.

Who wilt never cease to pour forth the streams of mercy. Blessed be Thou, life-giving Victim, Who for me, and the whole human race, wert offered on the suffering cross. Blessed be thou, holy and precious Blood, which didst flow from the wounds of my crucified Lord Jesus Christ, and didst wash away the sins of the whole world. Remember, Lord, Thy creature, whom Thou hast redeemed with Thine own Blood. I repent me that I have sinned, I long to amend what I have done. Take from me, then, most merciful Father, all my iniquities and sins, that purified in mind and body I may be made worthy worthily to taste the Holy of holies; and grant that this sacred foretaste of Thy Body and Blood which I, unworthy, purpose to take, may be the remission of my sins, the perfect cleansing of my offences, the scaring away of all foul thoughts, the renewal of all good desires, the healthful effectuating of works well pleasing unto Thee, the most firm protection of soul and body against the wiles of my enemies. Amen.

God the Father, God the Son, God the Holy Ghost, be with me and with mine, now and at the hour of death. Amen.

BEFORE HOLY COMMUNION.

At Evening Prayer.

In the Name of the Father, and of the Son, and of the Holy Ghost. Amen.

℣. O God, make speed to save me;
℟. O Lord, make haste to help me.

Ant. I will run the way of Thy commandments, when Thou hast set my heart at liberty.

PSALM 119. *Adhæsit pavimento.*

My soul cleaveth to the dust: O quicken thou me, according to thy word.

I have acknowledged my ways, and thou heardest me: O teach me thy statutes.

Make me to understand the way of thy commandments: and so shall I talk of thy wondrous works.

My soul melteth away for very heaviness: comfort thou me according unto thy word.

Take from me the way of lying: and cause thou me to make much of thy law.

I have chosen the way of truth: and thy judgements have I laid before me.

I have stuck unto thy testimonies: O Lord, confound me not.

I will run the way of thy commandments: when thou hast set my heart at liberty.

Glory be, &c.

Ant. I will run.

Chap. Therefore, my beloved brethren, be ye stedfast, unmoveable, always abounding in the work of the Lord, forasmuch as ye know that your labour is not in vain in the Lord.
—1 *Cor.* xv. 58.

SATURDAY.

Lord, have mercy upon us.
Christ, have mercy upon us.
Lord, have mercy upon us.
   Our Father.

Let Thy love, O my God, so perfectly exhaust my soul, that I may for the future stedfastly purpose to lead a new life, that I may renew my baptismal vow, and hereafter live as a sworn votary to Thy love.

Whatsoever things oppose my desire and Thy command, O Lord, as . . . or . . . I seriously and sincerely resolve to shun, and that out of love to Thee alone. O that Thine abounding and effectual grace may in the virtue and union of this Sacrament assist the purpose of my will, of itself, Thou knowest, O Lord, so unstable and frail. Thine eyes see my imperfections; but of Thee is all my sufficiency. Amen.

O Lord, raise up (we pray Thee) Thy power, and come among us, and with great might succour us; that whereas, through our sins and wickedness, we are sore let and hindered in running the race that is set before us, Thy bountiful grace and mercy may speedily help and deliver us; through the satisfaction of Thy

Son our Lord, to whom with Thee and the Holy Ghost be honour and glory, world without end. Amen.

I desire, O gracious Lord, from this moment to renounce everything that may displease Thee, and resolve, through the grace of Thy holy Sacrament, to resist all temptations, and to become wholly Thine; for in my own strength I can do nothing; but on Thee I depend entirely, O my Saviour and best Friend. For Thy Name's sake, O Lord, for Thy love's sake, for Thy promise's sake, teach me whatever Thou wouldst have me to do, and then help me to do it. Teach me first what to resolve upon, and then enable me to perform my resolutions, that I may walk with Thee in the ways of holiness here, and rest with Thee in happiness hereafter. Amen.

God the Father, God the Son, God the Holy Ghost, be with me and with mine, now and at the hour of death. Amen.

SUNDAY.

CHRIST'S PRESENCE IN THE HOLY SACRAMENT.

Then we spiritually eat the flesh of Christ, and drink His blood; then we dwell in Christ and Christ in us; we are one with Christ, and Christ with us.

At Morning Prayer.

In the Name of the Father, and of the Son, and of the Holy Ghost. Amen.

Lord, lift Thou up the light of Thy countenance upon me this day.

HYMN.

Now, my tongue, the mystery telling,
   Of the glorious Body sing,
And the Blood, all price excelling,
   Which the Gentiles' Lord and King,
In a Virgin's womb once dwelling,
   Shed for this world's ransoming.

Word-made-Flesh, true Bread He maketh
   By His Word His flesh to be;
Wine, His Blood, which whoso taketh,
   Must from carnal thoughts be free;
Faith alone, though sight forsaketh,
   Shews true hearts the mystery.

Therefore we, before Him bending,
 This great Sacrament revere;
Types and shadows have their ending,
 For the newer rite is here;
Faith our outward sense befriending,
 Makes our inward vision clear.

Glory let us give and blessing
 To the Father and the Son,
Honour, might, and praise addressing,
 While eternal ages run;
Ever, too, His love confessing,
 Who from Both with Both is One. Amen.

Ant. Like as the hart desireth the waterbrooks, so longeth my soul after Thee, O God.

Psalm 84. *Quam dilecta!*

O how amiable are thy dwellings: thou Lord of hosts!

My soul hath a desire and longing to enter into the courts of the Lord: my heart and my flesh rejoice in the living God.

Yea, the sparrow hath found her an house, and the swallow a nest where she may lay her young: even thy altars, O Lord of hosts, my King and my God.

Blessed are they that dwell in thy house: they will be always praising thee.

Blessed is the man whose strength is in thee: in whose heart are thy ways.

Who going through the vale of misery use it for a well: and the pools are filled with water.

They will go from strength to strength: and unto the God of gods appeareth every one of them in Sion.

O Lord God of hosts, hear my prayer: hearken, O God of Jacob.

SUNDAY.

Behold, O God our defender: and look upon the face of thine Anointed.

For one day in thy courts: is better than a thousand.

I had rather be a doorkeeper in the house of my God: than to dwell in the tents of ungodliness.

For the Lord God is a light and defence: the Lord will give grace and worship, and no good thing shall he withhold from them that live a godly life.

O Lord God of hosts: blessed is the man that putteth his trust in thee.

Glory be, &c.

Ant. Like as the hart.

Chap. I am the living Bread which came down from heaven: if any man eat of this bread, he shall live for ever: and the bread that I will give is My Flesh, which I will give for the life of the world.—*S. John* vi. 51.

>Lord, have mercy upon us.
>Christ, have mercy upon us.
>Lord, have mercy upon us.
>
>Our Father.

O Lord God, in whatever from infancy until this day, knowingly or unknowingly, inwardly or outwardly, sleeping or waking, by words, deeds, or thoughts, by the darts of fiery enemies, or by the desires of my unclean heart, I have sinned against Thee, pity me, and remit to me, for the sake of Jesus Christ our Lord. Amen.

O Lord Jesus, I come to Thee, I come trusting to no righteousness of my own; I am blind, for I cannot see good things; I am lame, for I cannot walk on the right road; I am deaf, for I cannot hear Thy Holy Word aright; I am dumb, for I cannot speak of Thee as I ought; I am naked, for my own righteousnesses are but as rags, filthy rags; I am barren, for I bring forth a miserable harvest of good fruits, and not as I ought to do. Here, then, I am, O Lord, this morning; I am going to Thy holy altar; I confess that I shall kneel there deaf, dumb, naked, and barren, yet, Lord, I am going to Thee; I want sight, soundness, hearing, voice, clothing, fruitfulness in well-doing; I want them, Lord, but only from Thee. I do not wish to be troubled because I have them not, for I would rather have them from Thee. Thus then I come; emptied quite; emptied of myself, emptied utterly, begging Thee to fill me, to fill me with Thine own Self; to wash my soiled robes in the Blood of Thy Sacrifice. I come to Thee in the Sacrament of Thy most blessed Body and Blood as to the foot of Thy Cross. O Lord, as Thou didst suffer a poor penitent with unclean lips to kiss Thy feet at supper, and to stand all cleansed beside Thy Cross on Calvary; so suffer me, all trembling with my conscious guilt, to touch Thee through the Sacrament of Thine Atonement, lest I die. Amen.

O Jesu, Bread of Life, lo, my soul waiteth for Thee, send me not away fasting, lest I faint by the way.
O Jesu, Fountain of Life, my soul thirsteth after Thee; O let me draw water with joy out of the wells of salvation.
O Jesu, Beloved, fairer than the sons of men, draw me after Thee with the cords of Thy love.
O Jesu, jealous for souls, Whose delight is to be with the sons of men, may I love Thee, and all in and for Thee. Amen.

God the Father, God the Son, God the Holy Ghost, be with me and with mine, now and at the hour of death. Amen.

AFTER HOLY COMMUNION.

time I have uttered against Thy will, or caused others to utter. O most sweet Jesu Christ, I, unworthy sinner, yet redeemed by Thy precious Blood, call to Thy memory all the good works which, for our salvation, Thou wroughtest in the earth. I beseech Thee, most piteous Lord, pardon me whatsoever, by my ill-doing, I have, knowingly or unknowingly, committed against Thy law, and the glory of Thy Name, or have caused others to commit. And now, O most kind Lord, direct and order all my thoughts, words, and works, according to Thy good pleasure, to the praise of Thy Name; and conform them to the perfect rule of Thy most holy life and conversation. Thine I am, O Lord, and will be, in life and in death; into Thy hands I commend myself, and all that I am.

Purge me with the hyssop of Thy Blood, and I shall be clean. Wash me, and I shall be whiter than snow.

O Jesu, Saviour of the world, Who camest to save sinners, and saidst, Come unto Me, all ye that labour and are heavy laden, and I will refresh you; lo, I a sinner dare to come unto Thee, for with Thee there is plenteous redemption. I come unto Thee, from Whom I have erred and strayed as a sheep that is lost; but

After Holy Communion.

SUNDAY.

At Evening Prayer.

IN the Name of the Father, and of the Son, and of the Holy Ghost. Amen.

Glory be to the Father, and to the Son : and to the Holy Ghost :

As it was in the beginning, is now, and ever shall be : world without end. Amen.

Ant. Thou hast anointed my head with oil, and my cup shall be full.

PSALM 23. *Dominus regit me.*

The Lord is my shepherd : therefore can I lack nothing.

He shall feed me in a green pasture : and lead me forth beside the waters of comfort.

He shall convert my soul : and bring me forth in the paths of righteousness, for his Name's sake.

Yea, though I walk through the valley of the shadow of death, I will fear no evil : for thou art with me ; thy rod and thy staff comfort me.

Thou shalt prepare a table before me against them that trouble me : thou hast anointed my head with oil, and my cup shall be full.

But thy loving-kindness and mercy shall follow me all the days of my life : and I will dwell in the house of the Lord for ever.

Glory be, &c.

Ant. Thou hast anointed.

AFTER HOLY COMMUNION.

Chap. Whoso eateth My Flesh and drinketh My Blood, hath eternal life, and I will raise him up at the last day.—*S. John* vi. 54.

 Lord, have mercy upon us.
 Christ, have mercy upon us.
 Lord, have mercy upon us.
  Our Father.

I render Thee thanks, O Lord, Holy Father, Almighty, Everlasting God, Who hast vouchsafed, not for any desert of mine, but only out of the condescension of Thy mercy, to feed me, a sinner, Thy unworthy servant, with the precious Body and Blood of Thy Son, our Lord Jesus Christ; and I pray that this Holy Communion may not bring guilt upon me to condemnation, but may intercede for me to my pardon and salvation; let it be to me an armour of faith, and a shield of good purpose; a riddance of all vices; an extermination of evil desires and longings; an increase of love and patience, of humility and obedience, and all virtues; a firm defence against the wiles of my enemies, visible or invisible; a perfect quieting of all my impulses, fleshly and spiritual; a firm adherence to Thee, the one true God, and a blessed consummation of my end; and I pray Thee that Thou wouldest vouchsafe to bring me, a sinner, to that ineffable feast, where Thou, with Thy Son, and the Holy Spirit, art to Thy holy ones true Light, full Satiety, everlasting Joy, Pleasure consummated, and perfect Happiness ; through the Same our Lord Jesus Christ.   Amen.

O Thou Blessed Lord Jesus, Who hast this day vouchsafed to come under my roof, I most humbly beseech Thee, leave me not, but abide with me for ever. Abide with me, Lord, in all I say, think, do, fear, hope, and enjoy. I fear my own unstedfastness : abide with me, Lord, for in Thee there is no change. I often despond, and fear I shall fall : abide with me, Lord, and make me to feel Thy nearness. Be Thou my Refreshment in weariness ; my Comfort in trouble ; my Refuge in temptation ; in death my Life, in judgment my Redeemer. Abide with me always, that I may abide in Thee, O Good Jesu, Thou God of my salvation. Amen.

God the Father, God the Son, God the Holy Ghost, be with me and with mine, now and at the hour of death.   Amen.

AFTER HOLY COMMUNION.

MONDAY.

THANKSGIVING.

𝕿𝖔 𝕳𝖎𝖒 𝖙𝖍𝖊𝖗𝖊𝖋𝖔𝖗𝖊, 𝖜𝖎𝖙𝖍 𝖙𝖍𝖊 𝕱𝖆𝖙𝖍𝖊𝖗 𝖆𝖓𝖉 𝖙𝖍𝖊 𝕳𝖔𝖑𝖞 𝕲𝖍𝖔𝖘𝖙, 𝖑𝖊𝖙 𝖚𝖘 𝖌𝖎𝖛𝖊 (𝖆𝖘 𝖜𝖊 𝖆𝖗𝖊 𝖒𝖔𝖘𝖙 𝖇𝖔𝖚𝖓𝖉𝖊𝖓) 𝖈𝖔𝖓-𝖙𝖎𝖓𝖚𝖆𝖑 𝖙𝖍𝖆𝖓𝖐𝖘.

At Morning Prayer.

In the Name of the Father, and of the Son, and of the Holy Ghost. Amen.
℣. O God, make speed to save me;
℟. O Lord, make haste to help me.

HYMN.

At the Lamb's high feast we sing
Praise to our victorious King,
Who hath washed us in the tide
Flowing from His pierced side;
Praise we Him, Whose love Divine
Gives His guests His Blood for wine,
Gives His Body for the feast:
Christ the Victim, Christ the Priest.

Where the Paschal Blood is poured,
Death's dark angel sheathes his sword,
Israel's hosts triumphant go
Through the wave that drowns the foe.

MONDAY.

Praise we Christ, Whose Blood was shed,
Paschal Victim, Paschal Bread;
With sincerity and love,
Eat the manna from above.

Mighty Victim from the sky,
Hell's fierce powers beneath Thee lie;
Thou hast conquered in the fight,
Thou hast brought us life and light;
Now no more can death appal,
Now no more the grave enthral:
Thou hast opened Paradise,
And in Thee Thy saints shall rise.

Thankful triumph, thankful joy,
Sin alone can this destroy:
From sin's power do Thou set free
Souls new-born, O Lord, in Thee.
Hymns of glory and of praise,
Father, unto Thee we raise;
Risen Lord, all praise to Thee,
With the Spirit ever be.   Amen.

Ant.   Who satisfieth thy mouth with good things.

PSALM 103.   *Benedic, anima mea.*

| Praise the Lord, O my soul: and all that is within me praise his holy Name. | Praise the Lord, O my soul: and forget not all his benefits. |

Who forgiveth all thy sin ; and healeth all thy infirmities ;

Who saveth thy life from destruction : and crowneth thee with mercy and loving-kindness ;

Who satisfieth thy mouth with good things : making thee young and lusty as an eagle.

The Lord executeth righteousness and judgement : for all them that are oppressed with wrong.

He shewed his ways unto Moses : his works unto the children of Israel.

The Lord is full of compassion and mercy : long suffering and of great goodness.

He will not alway be chiding : neither keepeth he his anger for ever.

He hath not dealt with us after our sins : nor rewarded us according to our wickednesses.

For look how high the heaven is in comparison of the earth : so great is his mercy also toward them that fear him.

Look how wide also the east is from the west : so far hath he set our sins from us.

Yea, like as a father pitieth his own children : even so is the Lord merciful unto them that fear him.

For he knoweth whereof we are made : he remembereth that we are but dust.

The days of man are but as grass : for he flourisheth as a flower of the field.

For as soon as the wind goeth over it, it is gone : and the place thereof shall know it no more.

But the merciful goodness of the Lord endureth for ever and ever upon them that fear him : and his righteousness upon children's children ;

Even upon such as keep his covenant : and think upon his commandments to do them.

The Lord hath prepared his seat in heaven : and his kingdom ruleth over all.

O praise the Lord, ye angels of his, ye that excel in strength : ye that fulfil his commandment, and hearken unto the voice of his words.

O praise the Lord, all ye his hosts : ye servants of his that do his pleasure.

O speak good of the Lord, all ye works of his, in all places of his dominion : praise thou the Lord, O my soul.

Glory be, &c.

Ant. Who satisfieth.

MONDAY.

Chap. Giving thanks unto the Father, which hath made us meet to be partakers of the inheritance of the saints in light.—*Col.* i. 12.

>Lord, have mercy upon us.
>Christ, have mercy upon us.
>Lord, have mercy upon us.
>Our Father.

Blessed art Thou, O most merciful God, Who didst vouchsafe to espouse me to the heavenly Bridegroom in the waters of Baptism, and hast imparted Thy Body and Blood, as a new gift of espousal, and the meet consummation of Thy love.

Blessed art Thou, most pitiful God, Who in all my unfaithfulness and my sins, hast patiently borne with me, and prolonged my life even to this hour; and hast by Thy Body and Blood buried in oblivion all my sins; and hast happily engraved me in the remembrance of Thy most loving Heart and in all the bowels of Thy mercy.

Blessed art Thou, most glorious God, Who hast preserved me from many miseries and sins, and mercifully delivered me from those into which I had fallen; and by Thy Body and Blood hast graciously turned all my condemnation to salvation.

O most sweet Lord Jesu, transfix the affections of my inmost soul with that most joyous and most healthful wound of Thy love, with true, serene, most holy, apostolic charity; that my soul may ever languish and melt with entire love and longing for Thee. Let it desire Thee, and faint for Thy courts; long to be dissolved and be with Thee. Grant that my soul may hunger after Thee, the Bread of Angels, the refreshment of holy souls, our supersubstantial Bread, Who hast all sweetness and savour, and every pleasurable delight. Thee, Whom the Angels desire to look into, may my heart ever hunger after and feed upon, and may the appetite of my soul be filled with the sweetness of Thy savour. May it ever thirst for Thee, the fountain of life, the fountain of wisdom and knowledge, the fountain of eternal light, the torrent of pleasure, the richness of the House of God. Let it ever compass Thee, seek Thee, find Thee, stretch towards Thee, arrive at Thee, meditate upon Thee, speak of Thee, and do all things to the praise and glory of Thy holy Name, with humility and discretion, with love and delight, with readiness and affection, with perseverance to the end: and be Thou ever my Hope, my whole Confidence, my Riches, my Delight, my Pleasure, my Joy,

MONDAY.

my Rest and Tranquillity, my Peace, my sweet Saviour, my Food, my Refreshment, my Refuge, my Help, my Wisdom, my Portion, my Possession, my Treasure, in Whom my mind and my heart may ever remain fixed and firm, and rooted immoveably. Amen.

God the Father, God the Son, God the Holy Ghost, be with me and with mine, now and at the hour of death. Amen.

At Evening Prayer.

In the Name of the Father, and of the Son, and of the Holy Ghost. Amen.

℣. O God, make speed to save me;
℟. O Lord, make haste to help me.
Ant. Let everything that hath breath praise the Lord.

Psalm 150. *Laudate Dominum.*

O praise God in his holiness: praise him in the firmament of his power.

Praise him in his noble acts: praise him according to his excellent greatness.

Praise him in the sound of the trumpet: praise him upon the lute and harp.

Praise him in the cymbals and dances: praise him upon the strings and pipe.

Praise him upon the well-tuned cymbals: praise him upon the loud cymbals.

Let every thing that hath breath: praise the Lord.

Glory be, &c.

Ant. Let everything.

Chap. And they sung a new song, saying, Thou art worthy to take the book, and to open the seals thereof: for Thou wast slain, and hast redeemed us to God by Thy blood, out of every kindred, and tongue, and people, and nation; and hast made us unto our God kings and priests: and we shall reign on the earth.—*Rev.* v. 9, 10.

>Lord, have mercy upon us.
>Christ, have mercy upon us.
>Lord, have mercy upon us.
>
>Our Father.

I thank Thee, O Lord my God, that Thou hast not rejected me, a sinner, but hast permitted me to become a partaker of Thy holy table. I thank Thee that ,Thou hast enabled me, though unworthy, to receive Thy pure and heavenly gifts. But, O Lord most merciful, Who didst die for us and wast raised again, and hast bestowed upon us these awful and life-giving mysteries, to the salvation and sanctification of our souls and bodies; grant that, preserved by them in Thy holiness, I may ever call to mind Thy grace, and live not unto myself, but unto Thee, our Lord and Benefactor. And thus that when this life shall have passed

MONDAY.

away in the hope of eternity, I may attain unto everlasting rest, where the hymn of those that glorify Thee, and the joy of those that see Thy face for evermore, are unceasing. For Thou art the endless desire and inexpressible joy of those that love Thee, O Christ our God, and all creation glorifies Thee to all eternity. Amen.

What return, O Lord, can I give to Thee for all the benefits which Thou hast done unto me? Do I not owe my life, my soul, my body, my all to Thee, Who hast freely given me all, yea, Thy very Son Himself, Who for me laid down His life? Truly, O Lord, I owe my whole self to Thee, Who, to redeem me the guilty, didst give wholly Thy guiltless Son. O that I could present my body a living sacrifice, holy, well-pleasing unto Thee. I beseech Thee, O Lord, despise not Thou Thy servant, who hath nought to offer Thee more pleasing than Him in whom Thou art well pleased, and then bringeth Thee two mites, my soul and body, which I wholly make over to Thy service and Thy good pleasure. Amen.

God the Father, God the Son, God the Holy Ghost, be with me and with mine, now and at the hour of death. Amen.

TUESDAY.

PERSEVERANCE.

Following the commandments of God, and walking from henceforth in His holy ways.

At Morning Prayer.

In the Name of the Father, and of the Son, and of the Holy Ghost. Amen.

℣. O God, make speed to save me;
℟. O Lord, make haste to help me.

Hymn.

O help us, Lord ! each hour of need
    Thy heavenly succour give ;
Help us in thought, and word, and deed,
    Each hour on earth we live.

O help us, when to Thee we cry
    With contrite anguish sore ;
And when our hearts are cold and dry,
    O help us, Lord, the more !

TUESDAY.

O help us, through the power of faith,
    More firmly to believe;
For still the more the servant hath,
    The more shall he receive.

O help us, Jesu, from on high—
    We know no help but Thee;
O help us so to live and die,
    As Thine in Heaven to be.

To Father, Son, and Holy Ghost,
    The God Whom we adore,
Be glory, as it was, is now,
    And shall be evermore. Amen.

Ant. He will not suffer thy foot to be moved, and He that keepeth thee will not sleep.

PSALM 121. *Levavi oculos.*

I will lift up mine eyes unto the hills: from whence cometh my help.

My help cometh even from the Lord: who hath made heaven and earth.

He will not suffer thy foot to be moved: and he that keepeth thee will not sleep.

Behold, he that keepeth Israel: shall neither slumber nor sleep.

The Lord himself is thy keeper: the Lord is thy defence upon thy right hand:

So that the sun shall not burn thee by day: neither the moon by night.

The Lord shall preserve thee from all evil: yea, it is even he that shall keep thy soul.

The Lord shall preserve thy going out, and thy coming in: from this time forth for evermore.

Glory be, &c.

Ant. He will not suffer.

Chap. To him that overcometh will I give to eat of the hidden manna, and will give him a white stone, and in the stone a new name written, which no man knoweth saving him that receiveth it.—*Rev.* ii. 17.

> Lord, have mercy upon us.
> Christ, have mercy upon us.
> Lord, have mercy upon us.
>
> Our Father.

O crucified Jesu, hide me in Thy wounded side; cleanse me in that precious Blood flowing from thy pierced heart, and fill me with Thy perfect love, that I may ever be seeking after Thee, my Lord and my Saviour. Conform my heart to Thee, that I may be Thine for ever, and may truly love all men in Thee and for Thee. O inflame my love, quicken my faith, rectify my intentions, strengthen my confidence in Thee, destroy all self-complacency, and establish me in all goodness and sanctity. So elevate my soul above all changes and accidents, that I may always realize Thy Divine presence, and be so absorbed in Thy love, that no outward things may trouble me, no inferior cares entangle me, nor anything impede the sweet influences of Thy Divine grace. Hear me, O Lamb of God, and help me, and be Thou my comfort during my earthly pilgrimage, and my sanctuary in the hour of death. Amen. Alleluia. Alleluia.

O most gracious God, I desire with all my heart to serve Thee henceforward in holiness and righteousness all the days of my life. O that my ways were made so direct that I might keep Thy statutes! Look, I pray Thee, on my infirmity with the eyes of Thy mercy, for without Thee I can do nothing good, but of Thee is all our sufficiency. Make Thou me therefore to go in the paths of Thy commandments, for therein is my desire. Give me understanding, and I shall keep Thy law. Try me, O God, and seek the ground of my heart; prove me and examine my thoughts. Look well if there be any way of wickedness in me, and lead me in the way everlasting. Amen.

God the Father, God the Son, God the Holy Ghost, be with me and with mine, now and at the hour of death. Amen.

AFTER HOLY COMMUNION.

At Evening Prayer.

In the Name of the Father, and of the Son, and of the Holy Ghost. Amen.

℣. O God, make speed to save me;
℟. O Lord, make haste to help me.
Ant. Let Thine hand help me, for I have chosen Thy commandments.

PSALM 119. *Appropinquet deprecatio.*

Let my complaint come before Thee, O Lord : give me understanding, according to thy word.
Let my supplication come before thee; deliver me, according to thy word.
My lips shall speak of thy praise : when thou hast taught me thy statutes.
Yea, my tongue shall sing of thy word : for all thy commandments are righteous.
Let thine hand help me : for I have chosen thy commandments.
I have longed for thy saving health, O Lord : and in thy law is my delight.
O let my soul live, and it shall praise thee : and thy judgments shall help me.
I have gone astray like a sheep that is lost : O seek thy servant, for I do not forget thy commandments.
Glory be, &c.

Ant. Let thine hand.
Chap. To him that overcometh will I give to eat of the tree of life, which is in the midst of the paradise of God.—*Rev.* ii. 7.

TUESDAY.

Lord, have mercy upon us.
Christ, have mercy upon us.
Lord, have mercy upon us.

Our Father.

Grant, O good Jesu, by all Thy mercies, that I may ever honour this awful Mystery and wondrous gift of Thy love with due faith, reverence, and gratitude; and may I give diligence also to adorn the station to which Thou hast been pleased to call me, with charity, purity, humility, gentleness, patience, and sobriety, and with all such behaviour as is pleasing to Thee, and becometh a faithful servant of Thine. And all this, that my service may be more pleasing to Thee, to Thy greater glory, the good of Thy Church, and my own and my neighbour's salvation. Amen.

Abide with me, O Lord, and set Thyself as a seal upon my heart. Draw me, that I may run after Thee. Kindle in me the fire which Thou camest to send upon the earth. O that I might love Thee, O Lord, my Strength, my Refuge and my Deliverer. O that I could embrace Thee with that most burning love of Angels and of Thine Elect, so that nothing might separate me from Thee; for Thou, O God, art my Lot and my Portion for ever. It is good for me to hold me fast by Thee, for whom have I in Heaven but Thee, and what is there on earth that I desire in comparison of Thee? Amen.

O Lord Jesus Christ, to Thee I desire to consecrate all my thoughts, desires, affections, and my whole life. I have offended Thee enough, O dear Lord, in my past life: I would spend the time which remains to me in loving Thee as fervently as I can. Accept, O God of mercy, the Sacrifice which is offered Thee by this miserable sinner, who desires nothing but to love and please Thee for ever. Work in me, and dispose of me, and of all things which belong to me, as is most pleasing to Thyself. Let Thy love destroy whatever is contrary to Thy will, that I may become all Thine, and live henceforward only to Thy service. I seek not earthly wealth, nor pleasures, nor honours, but I ask of Thee, by the merits of Thy Passion and Death, a continual sorrow for my sins. Give me Thy light, that I may discover the vanity of earthly things, that so I may desire only what Thou wilt give me. Give me patience and resignation in all my afflictions, and in whatever opposes itself to my self-love. Give me humility and fervent charity. And above all things, I pray Thee to grant me perseverance in Thy grace unto my life's end, that so I may never be separated from Thee. O good Jesu, never let me leave Thee. Amen.

God the Father, God the Son, God the Holy Ghost, be with me and with mine, now and at the hour of death. Amen.

DURING THE CELEBRATION OF HOLY COMMUNION.

During Holy Communion.

If there is time before the Office for Holy Communion begins.

ALMIGHTY, everlasting God, vouchsafe, I humbly beseech Thee, to look down from the height of Thy Sanctuary upon this congregation, and graciously hear and accept the prayers of Thy Church, offered to Thee on behalf of us all, by the ministry of Thy Priest, through Jesus Christ our Lord.   Amen.

Have mercy on all Thy creatures, and on me, a miserable sinner.

Cleanse Thou me from my secret faults.

PSALM 116.   *Credidi.*

I believed, and therefore will I speak; but I was sore troubled: I said in my haste, All men are liars.

What reward shall I give unto the Lord: for all the benefits that he hath done unto me?

I will receive the cup of salvation: and call upon the Name of the Lord.

I will pay my vows now in the presence of all his people: right dear in the sight of the Lord is the death of his saints.

Behold, O Lord, how that I am thy servant: I am thy servant, and the son of thine handmaid; thou hast broken my bonds in sunder.

I will offer to thee the

sacrifice of thanksgiving: and will call upon the Name of the Lord.
I will pay my vows unto the Lord, in the sight of all his people: in the courts of the Lord's house, even in the midst of thee, O Jerusalem. Praise the Lord. Glory be, &c.

Before the Prayer for the Church Militant.

O Thou, who sittest on high with the Father, and art here invisibly present with us, come and sanctify these gifts here presented, and those also by whom, and for whom, [and the special purpose (or purposes) for which] they are offered : and grant that this Communion may be to us an increase of faith, that need not be ashamed, a love without dissimulation ; for the keeping of the Commandments, the nourishing within us of all fruits of the Spirit, the healing of soul and body.

Or,

Accept, O Holy Trinity, this Oblation, which, in union with Thy Priest, we offer unto Thee in remembrance of the Passion, Resurrection, and Ascension of Jesus Christ our Lord, that it may tend to our salvation ; through the Same our Lord Jesus Christ. Amen.

HOLY COMMUNION.

During the pause while Non-communicants are leaving the Church.

O Lord, I am not fit nor worthy that Thou shouldest come under the filthy roof of the house of my soul: because it is wholly desolate and ruinous; neither hast Thou with me a fit place where to lay Thine Head. But as Thou didst vouchsafe to be laid in a stable and manger of brute beasts, as Thou didst not reject the harlot, a sinner like unto me, coming unto Thee and touching Thee; nor yet the thief on the cross confessing Thee, even so vouchsafe to admit me, an habitual offender, miserable and exceeding sinful, to the reception and participation of the most pure, most excellent, quickening and saving Mysteries of Thy most holy Body and precious Blood. Hearken, O Lord our God, from Thy holy habitation, and from the glorious throne of Thy kingdom, and come and sanctify us.

Before the Consecration.

The Lord send thee help from the sanctuary, and strengthen thee out of Sion: remember all thy offerings, and accept thy burnt-sacrifice.

O send out Thy light and Thy truth, that they may lead me, and bring me to Thy holy hill and to thy dwelling; and that I may go unto the altar of God, even the God of my joy and gladness, and upon the harp will I give thanks unto Thee, O God, my God.

I will lift up mine eyes unto the hills, from whence cometh my help.

Wash me more and more from my wickedness, and cleanse me from my sin.

If there is time, Psalm 122.

After the Consecration.

My Lord and my God.

Prostrate I adore Thee, Deity unseen,
Who Thy Glory hidest 'neath these shadows mean:
Lo, to Thee surrender'd, my whole heart is bowed,
Tranc'd as it beholds Thee, shrin'd within the cloud.
I believe whate'er the Son of God hath told;
What the Truth hath spoken, that for truth I hold.
'Twas the Godhead only on the Cross was veil'd,
Here the manhood also is from sight conceal'd.
Both alike believing, Thee One Christ I own,
Suing, like the robber, at Thy mercy's throne.

Thy dread wounds, like Thomas, though I
cannot see,
His be my confession, Lord and God, of Thee.
Lord, my faith unfeigned evermore increase,
Give me hope unfading, love that cannot cease.
Oh, Memorial wondrous of the Lord's own
Death,
Living Bread, that givest all His creatures
breath !
Grant my spirit ever by Thy life may live,
To my taste Thy sweetness never-failing give.
Pelican most tender, Thine own children's
Food,
Cleanse my heart's uncleanness with Thy precious Blood.
Lo, one Drop, dear Jesu, all the world could
save,
From sin's foul pollution all creation lave.
Jesu, Whom now veiled I by faith descry,
What my soul doth thirst for, do not, Lord,
deny :
That Thy Face unveiled I at last may see,
With the Vision blest, my Lord and God,
of Thee.

O Most Gracious Father, accept this holy
Sacrifice at the hands of the Priest, in union
with that all-holy Sacrifice which Thy beloved

Son, throughout His whole life, at the last Supper, and upon the Cross, offered unto Thee, for me, for ——, and all for whom He vouchsafed to die. Look upon the Face of Thy most well-beloved Son, Whom we offer unto Thee as a Sacrifice of praise, of thanksgiving, and atonement; and by His Tears and Bloody Sweat, by His Groans and Sighs, by His Labours and Obedience, by His infinite Merits, remember and have mercy upon Thy Church, and upon the rulers thereof, all Prelates and Princes, all those who can most advance or hinder Thy glory and the salvation of souls. Let Thy Priests be clothed with righteousness, him especially who now stands at Thine Altar and prays for us. Grant that he may be holy, as Thou art Holy, that by the purity of his life he may approve himself worthy to minister at Thine Altar, and with due reverence may honour Thine all-holy Mysteries and the Majesty of Thy Name.

Remember also my parents, brethren, friends, and benefactors; all who have commended themselves to me, especially ——; those who have done me wrong, whom I have wronged, offended, neglected to assist, and those whom Thou willest, through me, to direct into the way of salvation. On all these have mercy,

HOLY COMMUNION. 109

O Father of mercies, as Thou knowest and willest, giving them grace most perfectly to please, fear, love, and glorify Thee, with the Same Thy beloved Son and Holy Spirit, now and for ever, world without end. Amen.

We pray Thee also, O Lord, Holy Father, for the souls of the faithful departed, especially ———, that they may obtain joy and refreshment through Him in Whom they have believed. Amen.

In presence therefore, O Lord, of Thy Holy Mysteries, mindful of the saving Passion of Thy Christ,
　His life-giving Cross,
　Precious Death,
　Resurrection from the dead,
　Ascension into Heaven,
　Session at the Right Hand of Thee, His Father,
　His glorious and dreadful Return,

We humbly beseech Thee, that receiving our part in Thy holy Mysteries, with a pure testimony of conscience, we may be united to the holy Body and Blood of Thy Christ, and receiving them not unworthily, may we retain Christ dwelling in our hearts, and ever be a temple of the Holy Spirit. Even so, Lord.

And make not any one of us guilty of these, Thy dreadful and heavenly Mysteries, nor weak in soul or body, by our unworthy partaking of the same, but grant that we may worthily approach Thy sanctifying gifts to our sanctification, illumination and strengthening; to relieve us from the burden of our many sins; as a preservative against all the assaults of the devil; as a correction and check of our evil consciences; for the mortification of our lusts; the keeping of thy commandments; the increase of Thy Divine grace; and for the possession of Thy Kingdom.

Holy Lord, Who restest in the holy, hallow us by the word of Thy grace, and by the visitation of Thy all-holy Spirit; for Thou hast said, O Lord, Be ye holy, for I am holy. Lord, our God, incomprehensible Word of God, consubstantial, co-eternal, indivisible, with the Father and the Holy Ghost, we adore Thee in Thy holy and spotless Sacrifice; One Holy, one Lord Jesus Christ, in the Glory of God the Father, to Whom be glory for ever and ever. Amen.

O Blessed Jesus, the God of my heart, and the Life of my soul; as the hart panteth after the waterbrooks, so doth my soul pant after

HOLY COMMUNION.

Thee, the Fountain of Life. O come, blessed Jesu, and take full possession of my heart for ever. I offer it unto Thee without reserve, I desire to consecrate it eternally to Thee; I believe in Thee; I hope in Thee; I love Thee above all things—at least, I desire so to love Thee; I grieve, for love of Thee, that I ever offended Thee. Pardon, forgive, atone, by Thine own Self. Amen.

O fire, which always burnest, and art never extinguished, encompass me, kindle me with holy charity. Amen.

O Lamb of God, That takest away the sins of the world, let Thy humility and patience be offered, in satisfaction for my sins. Amen.

O Lamb of God, plead before Thy Father the bitterness of Thy Passion, for my reconciliation to God. Amen.

O Lord, I am not worthy to receive Thee, but by the bitterness of Thy Passion, forgive me all my sins. Amen.

If there is time, Psalms 84 *and* 130.

At the Altar.

Lord, I am not worthy that Thou shouldest come under my roof.

I am my Beloved's, and His desire is toward me.

After receiving the Paten.

Abide with me, Lord.

After receiving the Chalice.

Let my sins be washed away in Thy Blood, O Lord.

For any special Petition at the Altar.

O Eternal Father, I receive this Holy Communion of Thy dear Son's Body and Blood, humbly beseeching Thee, because of It, in It, and with It, to grant me (———).

Returning from the Altar.

My soul doth magnify the Lord, and my spirit hath rejoiced in God my Saviour.

If there is time after Communicating.

Soul of Christ, sanctify me :
Body of Christ, save me :
Blood of Christ, inebriate me :
Water from the Side of Christ, cleanse me :
Passion of Christ, comfort me :
O Good Jesu, hear me :
Hide me within Thy Wounds :
Suffer me not to be separated from Thee :
From the malicious enemy defend me :

HOLY COMMUNION. 113

In the hour of death call me, and bid me come to Thee, that with all Thy Saints I may praise Thee for ever and ever. Amen.

Te Deum Laudamus.

We praise thee, O God: we acknowledge thee to be the Lord.

All the earth doth worship thee: the Father everlasting.

To thee all Angels cry aloud: the Heavens, and all the Powers therein.

To thee Cherubin, and Seraphin: continually do cry,

Holy, Holy, Holy: Lord God of Sabaoth;

Heaven and earth are full of the Majesty: of thy Glory.

The glorious company of the Apostles: praise thee.

The goodly fellowship of the Prophets: praise thee.

The noble army of Martyrs: praise thee.

The holy Church throughout all the world: doth acknowledge thee;

The Father: of an infinite Majesty;

Thine honourable, true: and only Son!

Also the Holy Ghost: the Comforter.

Thou art the King of Glory: O Christ.

Thou art the everlasting Son: of the Father.

When thou tookest upon thee to deliver man: thou didst not abhor the Virgin's womb.

When thou hadst overcome the sharpness of death: thou didst open the Kingdom of Heaven to all believers.

Thou sittest at the right hand of God: in the glory of the Father.

I am my Beloved's, and my Beloved is mine. He feedeth among the lilies.

Let Him kiss me with the kisses of His mouth; for Thy love is better than wine.

Draw me, we will run after Thee: the King hath brought me into His chambers; we will be glad and rejoice in Thee, we will remember Thy love more than wine; the upright love Thee.

Mine own vineyard have I not kept.

My Beloved is white and ruddy, the Chiefest among ten thousand. Yea, He is altogether lovely.

Set me as a seal upon Thine Heart, as a seal upon Thine Arm.

I adore Thee, O great God, I adore Thee with the most profound, with the deepest veneration of which I am capable. I acknowledge Thee for my God, my King, my Redeemer, and my All. I confess that Thou art the Sovereign Lord over all things, that Thou art the God Who alone reigns in the Heavens and on the earth; that all things depend on Thee, have received their being from Thee, and subsist only through Thy power. I exalt, I praise and glorify for ever Thy holy and adorable Name. I unite with all the Saints, and all the Angels of Heaven, and all the just on earth, to adore, praise, and glorify Thee with them, and by them, for everlasting ages. Amen.

Behold, Lord, I have Thee now, Who hast all things; I possess Thee, Who possessest all things, and canst do all things; therefore, O

HOLY COMMUNION. 115

my God and my All, do Thou wean my heart from all other things beside Thee, for in them there is nothing but vanity and vexation of spirit; on Thee alone may my heart be fixed; in Thee be my rest, for in Thee is my treasure, in Thee is the sovereign Truth, and true Happiness, and eternal Life.

Let my soul, O Lord, feel the sweetness of Thy Presence. May it taste how sweet Thou art, O Lord, that attracted by love of Thee, it may seek for nothing wherein to rejoice out of Thee, for Thou art the joy of my heart, my God, and my Portion for ever.

Thou art the Physician of my soul, Who with Thine own stripes hast healed our sickness. I am that sick soul whom Thou camest from Heaven to heal; heal my soul, therefore, for I have sinned against Thee.

Thou art the good Shepherd, Who hast laid down Thy Life for Thy sheep. Behold, I am that sheep which was lost, and yet Thou deignest to feed me with Thy Body and Blood; lay me now upon Thy shoulders. What wilt Thou deny me, Who hast given Thyself unto me? O be Thou my Shepherd, and I shall lack nothing in the green pasture wherein Thou feedest me, until I am brought to the pastures of eternal life.

O Thou true Light, Which enlightenest every man that cometh into the world, enlighten mine eyes, that I sleep not in death.

O Fire, continually burning and never-failing! behold how lukewarm and cold I am. O do Thou inflame my reins and my heart, that they may be on fire with the love of Thee. For Thou comest to send fire on the earth, and what wilt Thou, but that it be kindled?

O King of Heaven and earth, rich in pity! behold I am poor and needy. Thou knowest what I most require; Thou alone art able to enrich and help me: help me, O God, and out of the treasure of Thy goodness, succour Thou my needy soul.

O my Lord and my God! behold I am Thy servant; give me understanding, and kindle my affection, that I may know and do Thy will.

Thou art the Lamb of God, the Lamb without spot, Who takest away the sins of the world; take away from me whatever hurteth me, and displeaseth Thee; and give me what Thou knowest to be pleasing to Thee, and good for me.

Thou art my Love and all my Joy; Thou art my God and my All; Thou art the Portion

HOLY COMMUNION. 117

of mine inheritance, and of my cup; Thou art He Who shall maintain my lot.

O my God and my All! May the sweet and burning power of Thy Love, I beseech Thee, absorb my soul, that I may die unto the world for the love of Thee, Who for the love of me hast vouchsafed to die upon the Cross, O my God and my All! Amen.

I beseech Thee, O most sweet Lord Jesu Christ, that Thy Passion may be unto me virtue, whereby I may be fenced, protected, and defended. Let Thy Wounds be to me meat and drink, whereby I may be fed, inebriated, and delighted. Let the sprinkling of Thy Blood be to me the washing away of all my sins. Let Thy death be to me everlasting glory, both now and for ever. Amen.

If there is time, any of the following Psalms: —103*rd*, 23*rd*, 118*th*, 113*th*, 134*th*, 150*th*.

After the Blessing.

O most merciful God, Who hast not disdained to admit us miserable sinners, even at this solemn hour, into Thy Presence, to glorify and praise Thee; forgive me all the failings which have come upon me, in this very time of prayer, in that other thoughts have taken hold upon me, and that I have not been duly watchful against sin ; through Jesus Christ our Lord. Amen.

Or,

It is finished and perfected, so far as in us lies—

The Mysteries of Thy dispensation,
O Christ, our God !
We have celebrated the Memorial of Thy Death ;
Have seen the Type of Thy Resurrection ;
Have been filled with Thine endless Life ;
Have enjoyed Thy ever-satisfying Dainties :
Whereof vouchsafe to make us all partakers in the world to come.

The good Lord pardon every one that prepareth his heart to seek the Lord God of his fathers, though he be not cleansed according to the purification of the Sanctuary. Amen.

PRINTED BY MESSRS. PARKER, CORNMARKET, OXFORD.

www.ingramcontent.com/pod-product-compliance
Lightning Source LLC
Chambersburg PA
CBHW022140160426
43197CB00009B/1375